PICTORIAL HISTORY of GALSTON

James Mair

Dear John
Thought you'd like this book
Love Kay.

COVER:
Oil Painting of old Galston
by Hugh Rankin

First Published in 1988
by Alloway Publishing Ltd.,
Darvel, Ayrshire

Printed in Scotland
by Walker & Connell Ltd.,
Hastings Square,
Darvel, Ayrshire.

ISBN No. 0-907526-37-3

PICTORIAL HISTORY of GALSTON

James Mair

INTRODUCTION

This pictorial history, the second in the series on the Irvine Valley, is intended to present aspects of Galston and its people. The writer is an inveterate admirer of past generations of the Irvine Valley, and a student of their lives. Old photographs help in this study, but many gaps occur in the record, as each generation seems to have carried out regular and systematic spring cleanings of written and photographic material, especially around the time of family flittings.

Heirlooms and keepsakes used to find a dusty home at the bottom of a press, in a loft, or even in stoup holes when these still existed, but modern houses provide few places for valuable historical debris to accumulate for long.

Inasmuch as this is a book about a place, it is about the recollection of persons and buildings, streets and playgrounds, groups and activities retained in our memory; of people we admired, places we liked to visit or live in, or even of fleeting experiences which, for some reason or other, impressed themselves on our mind.

Many of the places to which we were attached, although deserving to be preserved, have disappeared, some through irreversible decay, and others through neglect, or uncertainty about their value to the social and cultural good of the community.

Also gone are most of the old Galston people in these photographs, looking at us out of the past, and with them much of the energy and expressiveness of the old Scottish tongue, universally practised by them. How many today can still savour this description of weavers from a neighbouring town by the Galston character Davie Elshander:

> Man when I meet the weavers takin' their dinner hour walk, altho I may hae taen my dinner as weel's I can tak it, I turn hungry as sune as I luk at them! Jist tae see them comin' mairching alang wi' their aprons roun their waists, a dreep at their nose, and their lang blue shacklebanes hingin' ahint them, an a' chowin ravelins.

Elshander, known as the King of the Cadgers (itinerant pedlars of small articles), could be equally colourful in his dealings with the farmers:

> The best time tae cadge kintra-folk, is on the Fair Days, efter the Fair's bye, when their comin' oot o' a public hoose, smokin' a new pipe, an gaun awa hame. Man, I can cadge them fine then, but if I tak them in the mornin', when their fresh aff the heather, I micht as weel try tae cadge a stane wa'.

Even the parish minister last century could intimate the houses he would visit in the coming week in the following fashion:

> Straith and the Straith Mill, Staneygate and Winnyhill, The Mo'ment and the Mo'ment End, and the wee hoose ayont the hill, its name I dinna ken.

It can give a feeling of continuity or, in the modern idiom, 'of belonging' to know that the town and its streets have been there for centuries, and that people have lived and worked in them – people not very different from ourselves. Probably they were more independent and self-reliant, maybe even more sociable and compassionate. Their struggles were of a different order from ours, but it is to be hoped we face up to ours with as stout a heart.

The author thanks Alex. Kay, James Fulton and John Alexander who gave much of their time and assistance tracing old photographs and information. He also thanks all those who gladly offered prints for copying, or who helped in other ways towards the completion of this pictorial history, including; Mrs A Baird, Mrs J Bell, W. Black, Edward Gorrie, David Grier, Andrew Holland, George Hood, J. Stewart McLauchlan, Miss A.M. McLaughlan, J. Bunting, Mrs Jean Murray, Mrs J. Muir, Robert Murray, Hamish Stevenson, Thomas Wright, Thomas Yeudall, Mrs M. Young, Kilmarnock and Loudoun District Council Museum Services, the Ordnance Survey and the Royal Museum of Scotland.

HISTORICAL SKETCH

In 1811 Galston was described as one of the handsomest villages in Ayrshire. It was then on the verge of great social and economic changes as it was transformed from a small agricultural centre into a busy mining town. Its exact origins are lost in the distant past but it has the distinction of being the oldest surviving settlement in the upper Irvine Valley. Its name means 'the place of the strangers,' from the Gaelic word gall: a stranger, and the Anglian word tun: a hamlet or enclosure. As a hybrid word it is similar to other place-names in the parish which combine Gaelic, Cymric, Old Norse or Anglian. In its earliest written form- Gallistoun, the name suggests a time when there was a ferment of peoples and a mixture of languages in the area.

Gall also occurs in Gallisholmes, 'The meadows of the strangers,' the low lying ground west of the town, and in Gallalaw, 'the hill of the strangers,' later known as Molmont Hill. Who these strangers were it is now difficult to ascertain, but they were most likely the Gall Ghaidhil, 'the foreign Gaels,' who colonised this part of the old British kingdom of Strathclyde and left traces of their occupation in the numerous Gaelic names in Galston Parish. These are common among the farms such as Auchinbart- the field of the poet; Drumdroch- the dark ridge; Sornbeg- the small kiln; Liffnock- the grey hill; and Glenshay- the glen of peace or the truce; but which truce it refers to, or who agreed to it, is now lost in antiquity. It is not only in the upland farms that hints of the Gaelic tongue remain, but in and around the town itself in Barr, Clockston, Gauchalland and Kilknowe, known in their present form after all the languages of earlier peoples have been assimilated into modern Scots.

The linguistic boundary of the Gaelic language, lasting probably into the Middle Ages, lay along the western edge of Galston parish. It was marked by the Water of Cessnock, that is the Water of the Sasunnachs. In this case not the sasunnachs of the 8th century Anglican invasion of Kyle, but the Anglo-Norman immigration of the 12th and 13th centuries. Westwards beyond the Cessnock are the parishes of Riccarton and Symington, named after the Anglo-Norman knights Richard Wallace and Simon Lockhart. It was from this time, with the large influx of Anglo-Normans with their retainers and clergy, that the Celtic languages of Ayrshire began to decline, and what was to become the lowland Scots tongue emerged predominant. The lands of Galston and Loudoun parish ultimately, through marriage or by charter, became mainly Scoto-Norman possessions.

Galston became an important ecclesiastical centre after the feudal system was imposed upon the people of lowland Scotland in the 12th and 13th centuries. This was done under the direction of the monarchy and through the agency of the aristocracy and the church. The parish church of Galston was established by the Trinitarian Order of Friars from the monastery of Fail (or Failford as it was originally known), not long after its foundation in 1252, although it is possible the old Celtic form of Christianity had a church and possessions in the district before that time. The name Lanfine, from Lann Fionn, means a sanctified or consecrated enclosure, and as late as 1489 John Charteris, chaplain of Galston, obtained a letter of confirmation for these lands.

The Trinitarian Friars were a minor order in Scotland, established for the redemption of captives taken by the Saracens during the Crusades. Only three parish churches in Ayrshire belonged to them, Barnweil and Symington as well as Galston, and as no great overlord held land in the parish, only lesser barons, the church was in a very important and influential position. The records of the monastery of Fail were lost to sight in the 18th century, leaving nothing certain about the extent of church lands in the parish of Galston, but various place-names are associated with pre-reformation times. Apart from Lanfine already mentioned, Burnawn or Burn Anne, with the name of the saint and mother of the Virgin Mary, runs past Molmont Hill and through the town. On its northern bank, below the farm of Middlethird, there was a holy well dedicated to the Virgin.

To the south-west an ancient track or road lay between Galston and Fail, only seven miles distant. On the right of it were the orchards and on the left the glebe lands of the church. Between these and the Burnawn lay St Mary's Holm with St Mary's Burn running through it, while further west the lands of Ladyard probably belonged to the church. At the eastern end of the parish the village called Priestland is situated, with the adjacent lands of Ladybrow. All point to an extensive area with ecclesiastical connections. The church itself was dedicated to St Peter, and a fair was held annually on St Peter's Day, 29th June. In the 15th century a chapel was endowed with attendant chaplain at the Tower of Galston (now Cessnock Castle), and dedicated to the Virgin. Buildings known as Chapelhouses, mentioned in 1736, could have been the last vestiges of this chapel, but no trace remains.

Further evidence of the great antiquity of Galston is found in the career of Sir William Wallace who achieved an early victory over the English in 1296 at Loudoun Hill, after passing from Mauchline Moor through Galston and Loudoun. An ancient tree, which survived into last century, grew outside the wall of Barr Castle gardens, and was traditionally linked with the patriot and one of his many escapes from his enemies. In 1307 king Robert Bruce on his approach to the battlefield of Loudoun Hill, encamped his army at Galston. This was at the beginning of his campaign to clear Scotland of the foreign invaders, and is described by Barbour in his poem 'The Brus.'

For they believed, both great and small,
That having won such fair success,
They now should fear their foemen less.
Meanwhile the king was staying still
At Galston near by Loudoun Hill
The country to his peace to bring.

The parish figured strongly in this period of history. The burgh coat-of-arms, which in one quarter has a heart clasped by a mailed fist, commemorates another episode during the wars of independence. Sir William Keith of Galston was an outstanding soldier of the time and the commander who prevented the re-occupation of Berwick by the English in 1318. After Bruce's death, the king's heart was carried on a Crusade to inspire the Scots in battle against the Moors, and was brought back to Scotland by Sir William Keith.

Later the Tower of Galston and its lands passed through marriage to the Hamilton family, and successively to Stewarts and Rosses, until acquired by the Campbells of Cessnock in the 17th century.

The fragmented nature of land ownership in the parish, under a number of lesser barons, explains the lack of development of a burgh within its boundaries with the patronage of a great family. The church remained a large landowner and the strongest influence on the community until the Reformation in 1560. As elsewhere in the country its possessions excited the acquisitive interest of local lairds. One of the most fanatical supporters of the reformers proved to be John Lockhart of Barr. His family had property in the parish since late in the 14th century, but had not come into prominence until he and his brothers Hugh and Alexander attached themselves to the reforming party, and in particular to John Knox.

In 1545 the Protestant martyr George Wishart had preached in Barr Castle under the protection of the Lockharts. Knox also preached there in 1556 as he was barred from Galston church by its last vicar, Alexander Arbukill. This might have been the same cleric who had disputed with Knox over the ceremonies of the church at St. Andrews in 1547. Knox concentrated his activities in Ayrshire for a while and Lockhart, who later assisted in the capture of strongholds on behalf of the reformers, acted as one of his bodyguards. He also had a leading part in more disreputable incidents, for he was tried in 1550 for 'stouthrief (theft with violence) and spoliation of sundry parish churches, religious houses and chapels of their eucharistic chalices, altars and ornaments of the mass; and also of casting down and breaking choral stalls and other stalls and glazed windows.'

The monastery of Fail was razed to the ground after the Reformation, following an edict of the Privy Council for the destruction of abbeys and monasteries. The virulence of the reformers in Galston parish might indicate that some resistance was offered by the adherents of the old church, but no more is heard after this of the vicar. The only reference to the monastery which remained in the popular mind was the scurrilous verse:

The Friars of Fail they made gude kail
On Fridays when they fasted,
And they never wanted gear enough
As long as their neighbours' lasted.

But three centuries of religious life built on the foundations of the earlier Celtic church had been swept away. The priests, monks and friars had to conform to the new order or find another occupation. The hospital attached to the monastery disappeared and the provision made for the aged and poor was lost. New systems had to be initiated in the reformed kirk, while trained clergymen were scarce on the ground. One who did conform was Ranken Davidsone who was installed as exhorter for Galston and Loudoun. This post was given to a person appointed, in lieu of a minister, to preach and give religious instruction. During the years 1567 to 1576 he baptised 'the bairns' and kept the registers for the two Valley parishes, stating that they were:

Written by me
Ranken Davidsone
extortar at ye Kirk of Galston.

The few remaining friars at Fail had difficulty collecting their revenues from the parish and like old soldiers quietly faded away. In the church records for 1570 occurs possibly the last reference to the monastery when two foreign-sounding names, perhaps of two old friars, Robert Munst and Robert Libard of Failford were attached as witnesses at the baptism of Johne Ross in Hanying (Haining).

Old practices died out slowly. In pre-Reformation times leading families in the parish had been jealous of their privileges and vied with each other for burial lairs within the church and closest to the altar. This custom was condemned by the General Assembly, but John Shaw of Sornbeg resisted the new law and assisted by an armed party of relations, servants and friends, broke down the kirk door and buried his wife's remains within the building. He claimed he had been given this dispensation in 1551 by the last vicar.

Precedence in burial rites was replaced by competition over the location of pews among the presbyterian lairds. Each strove for the most advantageous and prominent position near the pulpit, and early in the 17th century the lairds of Barr, Galston, Sornbeg and Cessnock had been provided with strategic places, and separate burial aisles. Lesser lairds, rising in the world, but well-connected, were in conflict with the kirk session from time to time, as in 1676 Matthew Campbell, lawyer in Waterhaughs insisted that a decision of the Lord Justice-Clerk in his favour be implemented, and that he be allowed to build 'a loft which may commodiously contain his family and retainers.'

The second half of the 16th century had witnessed the violent overthrow of the monarchy with the enforced abdication of Mary, Queen of Scots, in favour of her son, and of the religious troubles following the Reformation.

The 17th century proved no less turbulent as attempts to consolidate presbyterianism conflicted with the aim of Charles I to impose a uniform episcopal system throughout the country. While in the 16th century the clergy of Galston parish might have held firm to the last in the old faith, by the mid-17th century the clergy and people were as strongly attached to the new.

The church records give a full account of life in the parish around this time. A near complete list of the adult male population is available in a copy of the names subscribed to the National Covenant in 1638. At the head is the minister, Alexander Wallace and the chief families of the parish, Campbell of Cessnock, Lockhart of Barr, Stewart of Galston and Shaw of Sornbeg. In all there are 328 names attached, many soon to be involved in the invasion of England to help in the downfall of king Charles. Over the following half century there was a continual movement of armed men about the parish. Watchers were placed on Molmonthill to tend the warning beacon, and to be alert for others lit on hilltops in the west, to call out the Covenanting levies.

The Scots army entered England and occupied Newcastle when Charles I raised his forces against the people. During the two years 1640-42 the kirk records mention various examples of punishments of local men who had returned home without permission, or of collections for the wounded.

> January 31st 1641, Collectit for twa men commended be the General Assembly and Presbytery having one of them his arm shot frae him and the other his hand – 8 merks 10 doits. June 19th 1642, Quilk day Archibald Willock gave signs of repentance for perjurie in leaving his cullours and being fugitive frae camp in Ingland.

It was not always heroism or dedication to the cause that brought parishioners to the notice of the kirk session. At the height of the Marquis of Montrose's campaign on behalf of the king his forces were summoned to a rendezvous at Loudoun Hill, following a drive through Ayrshire exacting fines from landowners and burghs. James Findlay and John Brown appeared on June 16th 1646 to be rebuked 'for going to Bodellbrig quhen the enemie were ther, but denyed they stopit ther at all, and confessed that they bought a horse; lykwyse that James Finlay restored his to the owner of it, and Johne Browne has oblished himself to restoure his lykwyse if it be challenged.'

> June 23rd 1646 Qlk day compeirit Wm. Mortoune, for buying plundered goods from Kilmarnock, quho confessed he bought some wool, but nothing else, and likewise that he restored it to the owner....lykewyse compeired Geo Steinsoune for the same business, who confesses he bought a pair of old plyds, but he's not yet restored them, but he promises to restore them if they be awned.

The people were not always willing to turn out for army duty. When an attempt was made to mobilize in support of Charles I, the men of Ayrshire and Clydesdale met in June 1648 to resist the call to join the Scots army. The government forces under General Middleton moved towards Mauchline and dispersed a body of two thousand armed men. They included large contingents from Galston and Loudoun parishes under the leadership of their respective ministers, the Rev. Alexander Blair and the Rev. John Nevay. In 1651 after Cromwell defeated the Scots in battle at Dunbar, his army led by General Monk subdued the country. It was at this time Loudoun Castle came under siege and was occupied, after which only sporadic resistance occurred.

The session records refer to one of the small incidents of the period, when a skirmish took place on Molmonthill between Cromwellian forces and a small band of insurgents. These appear to have been a roving company in the district, as no names are given and there was no one to claim the dead.

> To Matthew Ross's wyf, as part of the payment for the lining cloth taken frae her tae be winding sheets to the two young gentlemen that were slain at Molmont End in this parish by the Englishmen. 8th August 1654. Also four days collections that wer not delivered untill this day, distributed thus, seventeen shillings to Agnes Mortoune in Galston for completing yr the peyer of the gentlemen's winding sheets; thirty nine shillings to the soldiours. 23rd August 1654.

After the Restoration of king Charles II in 1660 there was no respite for the people of the parish. Fines were exacted from householders, and soldiers quartered on them without payment. Between 1660 and the revolution of 1688 the people were continually persecuted. Many Covenanters were pursued for taking part in the battles of Drumclog and Bothwell Brig, and James Smith of East Threepwood was summarily shot by soldiers near the farm of Bank on the Burnawn. Horse and foot soldiers were quartered at Cessnock in 1678 and Sir Hugh Campbell, who defended and gave shelter to his tenants, was fined sums of £800 and £1,500 before he was eventually imprisoned and his estates confiscated.

The Galston minister, the Rev Alexander Blair refused to celebrate the anniversary of king Charles's return to the throne and was thrown into prison in Edinburgh in 1673. He was later released, but died in the following year, and his place was taken by an episcopalian curate. A day of reckoning was at hand for the persecutors when king James VII forfeited his throne in 1688. John Graham of Claverhouse, Viscount Dundee, raised a royalist army on his behalf. In the last muster of the Covenanting army over 200 men of Galston parish joined the colours, and of them 25 never returned from the campaign of 1689, which led to the death of Claverhouse at the battle of Killiecrankie and the end of the Stuart cause. At home, with the re-establishment of presbyterian rule, the curate, the Rev Robert Simpson, found he was no longer welcome. He was given time only to collect his breeches and, on a winter's day, taken from the manse, pushed across the river Irvine and out of the parish, and told he must never return.

Trouble occurred regularly in the 17th century unconnected with the struggle for religious freedom. That impetuous family, the Lockharts of Barr again appear in the public eye, in 1626, when George Lockhart promised 'obedience the next Sabbath according to ye act maid anent ye drawing of weapons in the kirkyard upon the Sabbath day.' The kirk session was kept busy in its attempts to regulate the activities of the community, acting as the civil as well as the ecclesiastical power. In 1635 it ordained that no more than twenty four in all, twelve from each side, should attend bridals and that the lawing (the expenses for drink and entertainment) should not exceed the sum of five shillings. They feared that weddings would also get out of hand and tried to form new rules to prevent disturbances, 'Minstrels and pipers who is at brydells is oftymes the cause of fighting and jarres, falling out amongst the people, therefore the Session has concludit that all pipers and uther minstrells be dischargeit frae brydells in tyme coming.'

Sympathetic consideration was given to the 'hostlers and changers of meit and drink within the claghan of Galstoune' who had petitioned against 'the holding and keiping of brydell diners, burials and baptismes diners in landwart (the country places) with other hostelers, to the hurt and prejudice of them within the same claghan.' It was decided that the provisions for all ceremonial dinners and festivities should be given only to the town's people of Galston. But even local folk were sometimes a problem. In 1637 the Session had to reprimand the indwellers of the clachan for 'delving turves in the laigh kirkyard and brecking ye sward thereof for mending their dyks and byr, necessyrs qrthrow there can no market nor repair be maid.' On two occasions the age old belief in the power of witches, spaewives and wizards arose. In 1640 a Galston woman was brought before the session for 'charming and using such-like devices with sick bairnes and beasts and dougs.' As late as 1724 a local man was rebuked 'for his scandalous and offensive behaviour in going to consult a supposed wizard in order to the discovery of goods stolen from him.'

The dreadful authority of the session over individual men and women throughout the 17th and 18th centuries in dealing with misdemeanours is made clear from an entry for 18th April 1675.

'Hew Wilson in Galston confessed to have perjured himself before the session... He is appointed and ordained the next Sabbath to stand in a sack cloth gown upon him in the juggs from the ringing of the second bell untile the next at the kirk door, and from there at the last bell to go to the public place of repentence in the same habit and there be publicly rebuked.' The juggs was an iron collar which fitted round the neck and was attached by a chain to the wall of the kirk or the tolbooth.

In 1640 there is the first mention of mining in the district when a poor collier, James Baird, received help, but the poor fund was greatly strained helping refugees from Ireland.

'To ane gentleman come from Ireland 11 shillings, 8 pence.' In 1642 fifty merks were collected 'for the help of those poor naked people from Ireland.' As late as 1644 'To ane gentleman's bairns come frae Ireland, 24 shillings.'

These payments were made in excess of the normal parish relief given to residents. They were donations given to casual poor as required, but who had no legitimate claim for immediate assistance. Galston records demonstrate a compassion for unfortunates, and examples of generosity which became a tradition in the community. When the Covenanting minister died in 1674 the kirk used the legacy for the benefit of the poor. 'The Session having formerly ordained two common coffins for the poor to be made, and they now being made, the price of the dails, iron work, and making thereof, extending on the whole to the sum of £11 5s 2d which J. Campbell is ordained to pay out of 200 merks by Mr. Alexander Blair.' The coffin for the poor, with a hinged lid, only carried the corpse to the graveyard. The coffin was kept for future use.

Galston at this time reflected the social and spiritual life of the people in the parishes of lowland Scotland. The influence and power of the church entered into and affected the lives of every person, and the strong arm of the church was the kirk session. By the middle of the 17th century, although still not officially raised to the status of a burgh, Galston began to acquire the appearance and functions of a small burgh town. In 1640 a bridge was built over the Burnawn to give access to houses east of the burn, and in 1650 the session, no doubt tired of the townspeople stealing turfs, sold a portion of the Laigh Kirkyard, and the area became the market cross.

Lacking a burgh council a baron court could be authorised and baron bailies appointed by the principal landowner of the parish. The first mention of such an official is in 1694 when a Bailie John Campbell was named as an elder of the kirk. It was not until the quieter times of the 18th century that the town of Galston began to grow on the basis of textile manufacturing similar to the neighbouring burgh of Newmilns. The speed of development can be seen in the increase of population from 455 in 1779 to 573 in 1791, while the scale and variety of domestic manufacture is inferred from the details in the Rev George Smith's contribution to the old 'Statistical Account of Scotland' in 1791.

There were 152 families with the following occupations:-

Weavers	55	Carters	3
Tambourers	24	Carriers	2
Shoemakers	21	Coopers	2
Stocking Weavers	11	Butchers	2
Tailors	11	Dyers	2
Wrights	11	Flax dressers	2
Masons	9	Horse dealers	2
Colliers	7	Gardener	1
Day labourers	7	Mole catcher	1
Grocers	5	Drummer	1
Lint millers	4	Baker	1
Sempstresses	4	Surgeon	1
Blacksmiths	4	Druggist	1
Paper makers	3	School master	1

The total listed is 198 and out of these 113 were occupied in the textile trades. The weavers made fine linen goods, but later in the century transferred to silks and muslins. The twenty four female tambourers were employed in the production of Ayrshire white needlework, while the lint millers and flax dressers manufactured linen thread from locally grown flax in mills at Longhouse and Burnawn. Other occupations of interest on the list are the three paper makers at Strath Mill, the eleven stocking weavers, and finally the twenty one shoemakers who formed the second largest group, making shoes for Kilmarnock merchants.

The early years of the 19th century witnessed a rapid rise in the population of Galston. By 1801 there were 905 inhabitants. In 1811 the figure had increased to 1351. The explanation lay in the huge expansion of the textile trades.

At the end of the 19th century the miners were regarded as the backbone of the working class, but at the beginning this position was held by the handloom weavers. From the date of the French Revolution in 1789 until the passing of the Reform Bill of 1832 Galston, like neighbouring weaving towns, was 'seething with revolutionary madness.' The first expression of anti-government feeling occurred in demonstrations against the terms of the Militia Act of 1797. The government intended to raise an armed force to help resist invasion. In defiance a Tree of Liberty was set up in Galston to show sympathy with events in France. As the baptismal records gave the dates of birth of men eligible for service, a mob broke into the house of the schoolmaster, who was also the session clerk, and carried off his registers.

A unique record of these times was kept in a diary by John Wallace, a weaving agent in the town, with entries from 1807 to 1832. He had represented Galston and Newmilns in 1793 at the Second Convention of the Friends of the People, a popular movement for reform. When this was suppressed he went into hiding for a while, but re-emerged to continue to agitate for democratic government.

During the early winter months of 1811 there was a depression in the weaving industry, which caused great hardship for the families in the Irvine Valley. Wallace tells how he 'assisted in ordering coals that were distributed to a number of people in the town, 38 carts of 4 creels, 18 carts of 3 creels and 2 carts of 6 creels being led by farmers gratis. Mrs Brown of Lanfine having sent five guineas, the remainder was paid off the money subscribed by the Farmers' Club, some of them having paid money in place of meal.'

At the end of 1812 the weavers claimed that their wages had been reduced by seventy five per cent since the beginning of the century. They went on strike and appealed to the courts which issued a list of minimum prices declaring them to be 'moderate and reasonable,' but the manufacturers refused to pay them. Wallace reported on January 4th 1813 that 'the weavers have decided to begin work today... having been seven weeks idle. Number of looms in this place, 237.' Conditions deteriorated further after the Napoleonic Wars. The nationwide weavers' association had been destroyed in 1813, the system of indentured apprenticeship had been broken, and the labour market had to re-absorb discharged soldiers. By 1819 in Galston 'several families appear to have no more than seven and a half pence per week for each individual... The prospect is gloomy as from every account trade will be little or nothing better through winter. Work is not scarce, but if those employed do not make a sufficiency to support their families, they may be driven to take unlawful methods and commit crimes, which in ordinary times they would abhor. Riots may be expected, and disorderly conduct of individuals looked for. A hatred of government will be expressed, as some of the laws passed lately were against the national voice, particularly the Corn Bill, the Dairy Bill and the Wool Bill.'

Popular demonstrations were held throughout central Scotland. One was held in Galston on October 23rd 1819. 'This day a public meeting to take into consideration the state of the country was held at the Barr, on the ball alley. A number of different places attended :- from Mauchline a party with a flag ; Kilmarnock a cap of liberty and four flags ; Newmilns a cap of liberty and one flag ; Darvel one flag. The number from the places might be :-Kilmarnock, including those who did not march with the banners, 1500 ; Newmilns and Darvel including stragglers 1200 ; Mauchline 100 ; from places not ranged under any standard, say 500 ; Galston town and parish, say 1500 men, women and children ; making 4,800 in all. The females of Galston presented a cap of liberty and a flag to the committee in the name of 270 female reformers, and gave a paper to the chairman expressive of their sentiments.' The red cap of liberty had been the symbolic headgear of the French revolutionaries.

With the country on the verge of revolution flags and banners were specifically banned by the authorities, but the men of Galston waved instead large Scots thistles as a demonstration of their patriotism and enthusiasm for reform, while Burns's song 'Scots Wha Hae' was adopted as the national anthem of a repressed people.

In the spring of 1820 the disaffected artisans were enticed into open rebellion, mainly through the work of government agents, and their small force of armed men was defeated at the battle of Bonnymuir. In Ayrshire eighteen of the leaders had been named and accused of treason, but absconded with rewards, ranging from ten to forty guineas, offered for information leading to their arrest. All but one were weavers, with five from Galston : John Goldie, Joseph Abbott, Alexander Roxburgh, Andrew Addison and Thomas Gray.

John Wallace lived to see the passage of the Reform Bill of 1832. It had failed in two earlier attempts in parliament and it became his opinion 'that a corrupt body will not reform itself, and that external force would be resorted to, before the end was gained.' The old radical at the prospect of a struggle then added 'that at one time I might have ventured myself, yet now I was too old.' When news of the passing of the Bill finally arrived over one thousand people from the Valley towns and the neighbouring farms, including 174 horsemen, paraded through Galston. The local instrumental band played 'Scots Wha Hae,' but seemingly had not available the music for 'The Muckin' O' Geordie's Byre.' Apparently, Geordie's Byre represented the corrupt government of the previous King, George IV. The Bill proved a disappointment, raising the number with the vote in Galston parish from 3 to 114. Working people were not enfranchised and while the new election was being held, with the polling station for the district in Barr Castle 'some ill-set young men from Newmilns occasioned some disturbance. Mr Gordon JP (of Milrig) was struck with a stone, and several constables had stones thrown at them.'

About this time the character and appearance of Galston began to change. It had grown beyond the old kirktoun by the parish church, confined to Old Manse Close, Brewland Street, Bridge Street, The Cross and Church Lane. The town was the centre of a thriving rural parish, enjoying the benefit of the new farming, with crop rotation, consolidation of farms, growth of root crops for winter feeding and lime spreading, introduced by the agricultural improvers. The woods of Lanfine had been largely planted in the late 18th century and early 19th century by John Brown, banker and manufacturer, and his successors until they covered 800 acres.

The landscape had also been transformed in the Cessnock estate by the 4th Duke of Portland, who encouraged his farming tenants to plant ash trees and provided a free supply of draining tiles from his tile-works. Earlier, while factor to the Earl of Marchmont, Bruce Campbell of Sornbeg had helped to develop the famous Ayrshire breed of dairy cattle. By 1837 cheese production had reached 210 tons annually in the parish as it settled down to specialise in dairy produce. That year the Rev Robert Stirling in his contribution to the 'New Statistical Account of Scotland' displayed his preference for the farm labourers who were 'still in the enjoyment of those high wages which the vicinity of manufactures generally produces, and being well fed, and not overworked, their condition is generally comfortable, and they are contented.' In contrast, the weavers who had formerly been accustomed to high wages had acquired in his eyes 'a taste for an expensive mode of living... Their condition, therefore, may now be reported as far from comfortable, and the discontent naturally arising from the state of things has been greatly increased by the ignorant or dishonest labours of political agitators.' The handloom weavers of Galston were fast approaching a universal attachment to the new movement for parliamentary reform known as Chartism. They were still the largest group in the community with 423 at the loom in 1837. The following year Joseph Hood of Newmilns started making jacquard machines and very soon almost every handloom in the Valley had one connected. Conditions improved and the number of weavers increased as the range of goods which could be produced by the jacquard loom widened and the demand for book and leno curtains, with their all-over floral designs, gave employment by the early 1860's to upwards of 600 weavers.

Before a branch line of the railway reached Galston, a stage-coach left the Loudoun Arms Inn every Wednesday at 6am for Glasgow, returning at 9pm Another left the King's Arms for Kilmarnock at 10am on Tuesdays and Fridays and returned at six in the evening. Goods were transported by carriers and the turnpike roads were busy with traffic bearing the textile produce of the Valley. Robert and Samuel Wilson sent a cart on Tuesdays and Fridays to Glasgow, coming back on Wednesdays and Saturdays, while William Robinson went every day to Kilmarnock.

Other textile manufacturers added to the growing prosperity of the town. In addition to a number of stocking makers there were four lint mills at the end of the 18th century producing linen yarn for the weavers. The largest belonged to Charles Blair at Kilknowe whose benefactions established an educational trust for the poor children of the parish. During the greater part of last century Richmond's Woollen Mill, employing up to sixty persons had a considerable trade in blankets, plaidings, druggets, sheetings and flannels, with outlets in Scotland, England and the colonies. The only trade in decline was in Ayrshire white needlework. Twenty four women had been employed in 1791 on the tambouring frame. Their numbers greatly increased over the next half century along with the expanding number of weavers, producing vast quantities of woven cloth. The simple designs had been developed into intricate lace insertions in cut muslin. Good wages were made by women working through the day and often sharing a lamp in the evenings. By 1856 fashion had changed and handsewing had been reduced to a few who, by necessity, had to work for three pence to six pence a day.

By 1851 the population had grown to 2500 and in ten years had increased to 3200. At the end of the 18th century the old kirktoun had been confined to an area within a stone's throw of the church. The first extension of the town carried it over the Burnawn into Polwarth Street and Dales Street (now Wallace Street), and by mid-century it had doubled in size on lands feued by the Duke of Portland. the new streets bore names connected with his family, Henrietta Street, Titchfield Street (previously Laigh Street) and Bentinck Street.

There seemed to be no clouds on the horizon, but within a few years the handloom weaving industry was struck a mortal blow. An embargo was placed on the export of cotton during the American Civil War (1961-65), and in Galston the weaving trade never recovered. Within a decade it was practically extinct, but while it withered the coal industry blossomed. It had modest beginnings on the estate of Miss Henrietta Scott of Cessnock. The first pits into shallow seams had been developed by John Wallace the previous owner, along with lime workings in the vicinity, but there were still only seven colliers employed in the district by 1791. Very soon the fatalities associated with this industry occurred, with perhaps the first being recorded in 1812 when 'Hugh Richmond who has for years wrought about the mouth of the coal pit, after he had let down the last of the men this morning, seems to have missed his footing, and fell down the pit, by which he was killed on the spot... The men below could not get the corpse up for near two hours,it being soon in the morning and no person on the coal hill.' This would have happened at a primitive type of bell-pit with miners being lowered and coal raised by a simple hoist.

The earliest use for coal, apart from domestic use, was fuel for the lime kilns, but by the second quarter of the 19th century demand had greatly increased to supply the growing industries of Ayrshire. In 1839 three furnaces had been erected on the Cessnock estate to smelt ironstone mined in the district, but remained in operation for five years only. It was mainly to exploit the rich seams of high quality coal that the Glasgow, Paisley, Kilmarnock and Ayr Railway opened a branch line to Galston in 1848, and by the late 1850's deep mining had begun at Streetheid Pit and Gauchalland. Old unemployed weavers were reluctant to enter the pits, but young men accepted this alternative employment alongside immigrants from other mining districts and from Ireland. While the neighbouring weaving towns of Newmilns and Darvel suffered from the dearth of cotton in the early 1860's the mining industry brought a renewed vitality to Galston and soon steps were taken to raise the town to burgh status. A rudimentary organisation already existed. In 1707 Sir Alexander Hume-Campbell, later 2nd Earl of Marchmont, had obtained an Act of Parliament for holding 'fairs and mercats' in Galston. In 1830 the Duke of Portland sanctioned the appointment of the two baron bailies, a clerk and elected council, but they had very limited powers and very few funds. The impetus to promote the town as a burgh came, not from aristocratic patronage, but from the inhabitants themselves. The long history of the town from the time it was named the place of the strangers in the old tongue, culminated in its creation as a Police Burgh in 1864.

The first minute book tells of the auspicious start of the burgh. 'At Galston within the Crown Inn Hall there upon the 6th May 1864 in the presence of Thomas Anderson Esq., Advocate, Sheriff Substitute of Ayrshire, convened the ten pound householders of Galston.' Until the passing of the Second Reform Bill of 1867, only those males with ownership of property with an annual rental valued at £10 per annum had the vote. This is clearly seen in the list of public spirited, but middle class, citizens who initiated the action.

Mr John Hendrie, Banker in Galston proposed the following gentlemen should be elected Commissioners for the purpose of carrying out the Act as far as adopted into execution within the Burgh viz :-

Mr Boyd Gilmour, Coalmaster, Titchfield Street.
Mr James Meikle, Orchard Street.
Mr Alexander Cochrane, Agent, Orchard Street.
Dr William Rodger, Bridge Street.
Mr Andrew Mair, Agent, Henrietta Street.
Mr James Meikle, Agent, Henrietta Street.
Mr John Mair, Merchant, Bridge Street.
Mr Robert Richmond, Woolspinner, Barr Street.
Mr Alexander Campbell, Spirit Merchant, Polwarth Street.

The Act made provision for lighting, cleansing, paving, draining and water supply and the early years were mostly concerned with these. Cleansing the roads, streets and syvers within the burgh was transferred from the Parish Road Trustees for an agreed payment of £5 annually. Some citizens objected to the sewer rate as they did not benefit from a connection, but the new council exerting its authority, dismissed all appeals. Public wells came under burgh jurisdiction and an inspection report stated that the ironwork of Mr Mathieson's pump was 'a little out of repair; the copper chamber of the Barr Street pump completely done, and nozzle broken away; the pump of Kilknowe Well not drawing water, all others in working order.'

The municipality eagerly set about its business. On June 13th 1864 the clerk was instructed to 'apply to the secretary of the Gas Company for terms to supply gas to the street lamps,' and by September had appointed Hugh Cowan, after ascertaining his qualifications and character, as street cleaner at a wage of fourteen shillings a week. Daniel Ferguson was engaged as lamplighter at six shillings a week and Matthew Taylor became the Town Officer. Meetings of the council were held in the Library Room, in Blair's School or in the hall of the Black Bull Inn. In November of the same year it was 'resolved to levy one penny per head on all cattle brought to fairs for sale, excepting on pigs which it was agreed to charge at the rate of one half penny per head.'

The growth of the mining industry was reflected in a minute of January 13th 1868 when 'dealers in gunpowder had met and resolved to limit their stock of gunpowder to the statutory quantity, but declined to contribute towards building a magazine.' The unco-operative decision of the dealers could have led to the next important consideration of the council, to take steps to form a fire brigade and the following, willing to act were enrolled :- John and Gabriel Steel, hosemen; John Roxburgh, assistant hoseman; John Robertson, John Mclean, Alexander Carruthers, Robert Torrance, Alexander and Robert Anderson, strippers; James Torrance, waterman; and John Reid, engineer. To become a burgh under the General Police and Improvement (Scotland) Act of 1862 a district had to contain a 'populous place' of over 700 persons. At that date Galston had 4427 within its proposed boundary and a parish total of 6331. As well as the other services the council had to administer the Public Health Acts. This requirement brought some interesting business before the council. Rule 6 for the town's common lodging houses directed that the Keeper 'shall keep the windows open from 10 to 12 o'clock in the forenoon of each day, unless prevented by tempestuous weather, or by illness of any inmate of such room.' All their efforts did not prevent an outbreak of smallpox in January 1874. The Sanitary Inspector, James Cunningham, reported that 'Peter Gear who had been under his charge as a patient had died the previous night and was interred at the expense of the railway authorities. That five new cases of smallpox existed in the burgh.'

The Public Health Acts seemed the most difficult to enforce. The drain from the slaughter house ran into St Mary's Burn, and the sanitary inspector, earnest in his work, had trouble with his superiors when he could not get his bill paid by the Convener of the Drainage Committee, 'when he caused a foul drain and cesspool to be repaired at Inkerman House.' He also reported that 'several fleshers and other parties were in the habit of killing pigs and other beasts at their back doors, instead of taking them to the slaughter house.' It was 'resolved to send through (the town) the Bell warning the inhabitants, and offering a reward of £1 to such person as will give information leading to a conviction.'

With a quickly expanding population came the problem of keeping public order. In 1864 the council applied to the County Police Commissioners for the use of constables stationed within the burgh 'to apprehend persons and bring them before the magistrates,' but it was not until 1867 that the Chief Constable, following an appeal to the Lord Advocate, finally accepted the proposal. Some of the local fairs and festivals could become unruly as Galston maintained its reputation down the centuries as a lively and colourful place. On October 27th 1886 the clerk to the council was 'instructed to frame a notice for the Town Crier at Hallowe'en warning parties against creating any disturbance in the town that night.'

By the last quarter of the 19th century Galston was best described as a mining town. Mr Boyd Gilmour, coalmaster, after whom Boyd Street was named, had been one of the sponsors of the new burgh and the largest number of male inhabitants were miners. The town outstripped its Valley neighbours in population and industrial expansion with one thousand miners in fifteen pits in and around the town, working the high grade coal of the district. The productive coal seams ran from Saltcoats to Newmilns, and half the coal produced in that area was mined in the vicinity of Galston.

The time of greatest activity occurred at the end of last century and the period up to the end of the Ist World War. The economic depression in the 1920s brought the great lock-outs of the miners in 1921 and 1926. Collieries were closed for many months, during which the pumps were not operating and pits were flooded. The best seams, where the main coal had been six feet thick, were exhausted and the mining companies did not survive. One after the other had opened up after the General Strike, and closed again, until the last at Maxwood was abandoned in 1933. Only two small ingaunees near Newmilns continued working for a year or two, but in 1935 with the demise of the Piersland mine three centuries of coal extraction ended in Galston parish.

Local men played a foremost part in the creation of the Ayrshire Miners Union in 1886 with Bailie John Brown and John Littlejohn active from the beginning. Keir Hardie the socialist pioneer was appointed secretary and within a year was agitating for better hours and pay, pressing for eleven days work out of fourteen and an improvement in wages which ranged then from two shillings and sixpence to four shillings per day. Living conditions were among the worst in Ayrshire and at the turn of the century thirty seven per cent of the families in Galston lived in single rooms, with only a few more enjoying the luxury of two apartments at a time when the number in families often reached double figures.

The old weavers' cottages in the town were later occupied by miners, and some were owned by them. Many of these still stand, while the miners' rows built by the coal companies at Maxwood, Gauchalland and at the west end in Boyd Street and John Street have been demolished. The most poorly constructed were the Loudoun Rows to the west of the town better known as the Taurry Raws from their round roofs covered with tarcloth in place of slates. They had no back doors nor wash houses, with communal water closets and ash pits set back from the houses. The floors were of brick tiles, which were often flooded by the nearby river Irvine, while ornaments vibrated on sideboards and mantlepieces when shot-firing occurred in the mine passages below.

Times were often hard for the families of miners. Soup kitchens had to be provided during the prolonged strikes, and on occasion badly injured and dead miners were carried home on a board from the pits. Nor was there much support from the Poor Law. As late as 1903 a widow with ten children was told by the Parish Council that it was 'unanimously decided to take you and your dependents in the County Council poorhouse at Irvine.' Soon after a widow with six children was informed that 'the poorhouse was for her and them at anytime they thought convenient.'

Other employment was available in the town in hosiery work, and Richmond's woollen mill was thriving. Two lace and madras factories, J.M. Robertson and Hendrie & Co., had been established and were competing with the numerous lace firms in the other Valley towns, where hundreds of Galston women and girls found work. As an agricultural centre Galston was well-situated with a large rural population, and most farmers were able to buy their farms at the break up of the Portland and Loudoun estates in the early 1920's.

It was in the period between the two world wars that the town faltered in its long upward progress. In the two decades before the Second World War, farming was not as rewarding as before. The pits closed and the textile industries were generally depressed with only spasmodic increases in activity. Yet this was a time of great improvement in the amenities of the town, when some of the poorest properties were demolished and families rehoused in burgh and county council schemes. This trend continued after the war and a whole new built up area stretched up the hill between the Kilmarnock and Ayr roads, while renewal projects for the old town continue to the present day.

The appearance of the town may have altered much, but the character of the people has not greatly changed. Circumstances shared in adversity created a close communal spirit, when only in the worst times did families have to look elsewhere than friends and neighbours for sustenance and support. Despite the disintegrative forces at work in the modern world, the old friendly traditions of Galston live on.

THE CLINCHYARD MOUNT

Dominates the landscape on the approach from the west by the Ayr road. Once the brow of the hill is reached, looking towards Loudoun Hill, the whole Vale of Irvine can be seen. Although not on the western boundary of the parish, it marks the beginning of the Valley for every Galstonian, and the view from it down into Galston remains in the mind's eye of the town's exiles.

GALSTON PARISH CHURCH

The first church on the site was dedicated to St. Peter and was built before the end of the 13th century as one of the five parish churches belonging to the Monastery of Fail. It proves the existence of Galston as a very early settlement. The present church was built in 1808-09, during the ministry of the Rev. George Smith (1778 - 1823) the great grandfather of Robert Louis Stevenson. He was also immortalised by figuring in three of the poems of Robert Burns "The Holy Fair," "The Twa Herds" and "The Kirk's Alarm."

The view here is from the area once known as the Laigh Kirkyard. It became the market cross, where the traditional stone cross survived into last century. The light patch on the wall marks where the lean-to shed once stood, which housed the local fire engine.

Parish Church, Galston

THE CHURCH INTERIOR

Before the numerous alterations which accompanied the building of the chancel in 1909. This was erected beyond the west windows seen here. The modern church, built a century earlier, retained the east-west orientation of pre-Reformation practice. Additional accommodation has been provided in recent years in the south-east corner, near the quaint and interesting gravestone commemorating the Covenanter, Andrew Richmond.

LOUDOUN CASTLE

Loudoun Castle has been the home of the Campbells of Loudoun for six centuries. The family played an important part in the early history of Scotland. Although based in the parish of Loudoun, branches had possessions at Cessnock, Mayfield and Waterhaughs in Galston parish. This lesser known view of the castle is the approach from the east, and behind the extensive remodelling lie two older structures, one dating from the 15th century. The castle was destroyed by fire in 1941. leaving an impressive but decaying ruin.

THE GATEWAY AND PORTCULLIS

The Gateway and Portcullis of Loudoun Castle were built when the structure was largely re-fashioned in the early years of the 19th century. This feature which stands to the east of the main building, was for decorative rather than defensive purposes and is now ruinous. Three of the large number of servants and retainers attached to the estate are seen here in the 1890's, perhaps the head forester, housekeeper and gardener. At that date the Loudoun family still owned most of the land in Loudoun parish, its farms, and the feus in the towns of Newmilns and Darvel. It had also owned the land around the site of the old castle of Auchinrugland in Galston parish, destroyed in a feud by Kennedy of Bargany in the 16th century.

THE ENTRANCE HALL

The entrace hall and stairway of Loudoun Castle showing the magnificence of the interior, which last century contained priceless treasures in sculpture, paintings and furniture. The library held over 10,000 volumes and a large collection of documents and manuscripts. Many historical relics associated with the family were on display, including, at the head of the stairs, the two-handed sword of Sir William Wallace. There was also a portrait of King Charles I which was damaged by Cromwell's soldiers after the siege of the castle.

LOUDOUN KIRK

Built in 1451, was the parish church of Loudoun until the early 17th century. It is now a ruin, apart from the choir, used as the burial vault of the Loudoun family. The building is today similar in appearance to that shown in the photograph from the 1890's. A pre-reformation structure, it probably replaced the original church founded by the monks of Kilwinning Abbey in the 13th century. By the choir wall is the memorial stone to Lady Flora Hastings who was maligned and broken in spirit by the young Queen Victoria. She was also commemorated by Lady Flora's School in Newmilns. Also in the kirkyard are the graves of the Covenanter Thomas Fleming of Loudounhill, and of Janet Little, minor poet, and contemporary of Robert Burns.

BARR CASTLE

Built in the 15th century was the family seat of the Lockhart family until 1670. Both the early reformers George Wishart and John Knox preached in the castle in 1545 and 1556 under Lockhart protection. This is one of the earliest photographs of the castle when the old tree, which seriously hampered the hand-ball players, especially visitors, still stood by its walls. The workshop and cottages which lay at a right-angle to Barr Street can be seen on the left, and on the right the schoolhouse of Glebe School.

TWO CHURCHES

Two churches can be seen in this print from the 1890's with Barr Castle seen from the east. The old tree by the wall has been removed and the area for the spectators at the big challenge games of hand-ball fenced in. The cottages at the end of Wallace Street were demolished after the 2nd World War. The Erskine Church (United Presbyterian) seen on the right is now the parish church halls. It was built in 1859 on the site of an earlier meeting house, dating from 1800. The steeple of Trinity Church can be seen above the trees. Out of an original total of five tower houses in the Valley only two remain in good condition, Cessnock and Barr.

CESSNOCK CASTLE

Formerly known as the Tower of Galston, is the last of the fortified houses in the Valley still in family possession. The main tower is of 15th century construction with the earlier parts at the lower levels. It once belonged to Sir William Keith, who brought the heart of King Robert Bruce back to Scotland, from the Crusades. The castle and lands came into the possession of the Campbells of Cessnock in the 17th century and the castle in time became known as the Tower of Cessnock. The bell on the keep (dated 1596) came from the old church of Galston. It was replaced by one presented by Sir George Campbell of Cessnock in 1696. The clock below the belfry is also believed to have come from the old church.

THE CESSNOCK SHOW

The Cessnock Show was one of the great-events of the farming year. Established by the Duke of Portland to encourage improved husbandry on his estate it rivalled the old established Newmilns Show. Held in the large field by the road into the Castle, it attracted the farming community, as here in the 1890's, from beyond the district and large crowds from Galston and other nearby towns. It lapsed early in the century and was not revived after the 1st World War.

THE ENTRANCE GATES

The entrance gates to Cessnock Castle at the beginning of the Century. The roads, paths, hedgerows and shrubbery were kept in excellent condition while the Portland family maintained a personal interest in the estate. The lodge house on the left is called Causeyfoot. Behing it lay the milldam which governed the flow of water into the lade to the sawmill at Burnhouse.

INTERIOR OF CESSNOCK CASTLE

Cessnock passed by marriage from the Campbells to the Earls of Marchmont. It then came into the possession of Miss Henrietta Scott, later Duchess of Portland. The 6th Duke greatly improved the property in the 1890's when this photograph was taken. The outward appearance of the building kept its character, but the interior shown here has an accumulation of Victoriana in contrast to the fine early painted ceiling. After the second World War the Campbells of Loudoun regained a connection with the castle.

MILRIG HOUSE

Apart from the Campbells of Loudoun and the Browns of Lanfine, whose policies covered large tracts of land on both sides of the Valley, there were a number of smaller estates around Galston. Some of the 18th century houses of the bonnet-lairds survive as at Sornhill Farm and Bruntwood, but the old house of Milrig was replaced by the mansion shown here in the 1890's. Large fortunes had been made in colonial trade at the end of the 18th century and the beginning of the 19th. The possession of land with a country house, became the ambition of newly-rich merchants and retired officers of the armed services, many of whom settled in Ayrshire. Modern taxation policies and the high cost of labour made the maintenance of many mansion houses untenable and, like Milrig house, were demolished after the 2nd World War or allowed to fall into decay.

RURAL PARADISE

This photograph of the gardener's cottage at Milrig early this century tells much about the changes in the Irvine Valley over the last hundred years. Like the mansion house of Milrig itself the cottage is now gone, along with the majority of the rural population. Then, each farm had a number of male and female workers; ploughmen and dairymaids. The Country estates had indoor servants; butlers and valets, housekeepers, kitchen and housemaids, and outdoors; coachmen and stableboys, gardeners, foresters and game-keepers, as well as day labourers employed when required. All have disappeared apart from the extra hand on the larger farms. Fortunately in the Valley there was not the rural poverty found in so many districts, and the country places shared the same air of prosperity of the three manufacturing towns.

HOLMES

The Valley has been unfortunate in the recent loss of so many public buildings in the towns and private houses in the countryside of historical and architectural interest. Holmes was bought at the beginning of the 2nd World War, stripped of its internal furnishings, and of its roof for its materials. It is now the ruined shell of the Tudor style mansion, built by Mungo Fairlie, who had made his fortune in trade with the East and West Indies.

The house is shown as it was at the beginning of the century. The area between it and the river had once been described as "a piece of the best land in the west," before it was undermined by the coal pits. In early times up until the mid 19th century these were the Gallisholmes - the rich holm-lands of Galston.

LONGHOUSE

Longhouse, seen here in 1894 belonged to the Blair family, who owned last century, with the exception of the Duke of Portland, the largest part of Galston. Their land known as Kilknowe or Lynn's Acre lay between the river and Henrietta Street, and eastwards from Polwarth Street to Blair Street and beyond. In the picture the old stable, behind the cart, still stands, but the thatched dwellings of Longhouse were replaced at the turn of the century by the sandstone buildings at 5-7 Barrmill Road. The last of the family, Charles Blair endowed a free school for poor scholars in the town. Blair's School was opened in 1841 and served the population until the end of fee-paying in state education fifty years later. The old school building survives in Polwarth Street, having been utilised as a post office, shops and dwellings in recent years.

KILKNOWE MILL

Kilknowe Mill was built in 1746 by Andrew Blair who later acquired the adjacent lands as his business prospered. It was established as a lint mill to which customers brought their flax from within a radius of ten miles to be heckled, and Robert Burns while in Mossgiel was one of these. It also housed a waulk mill and dye house for the preparation of wool used in the thriving bonnet-making trade in the town. Shown here in the 1890's when it had become a saw-mill, owned by the Yeudall family, it was still powered by water from the lade. The buildings were finally demolished between the two World Wars.

The two storey houses on the left were in Barrmill Road. Owned by Robertsons of the lace factory, and occupied by their workers. They were cleared away in the 1960's.

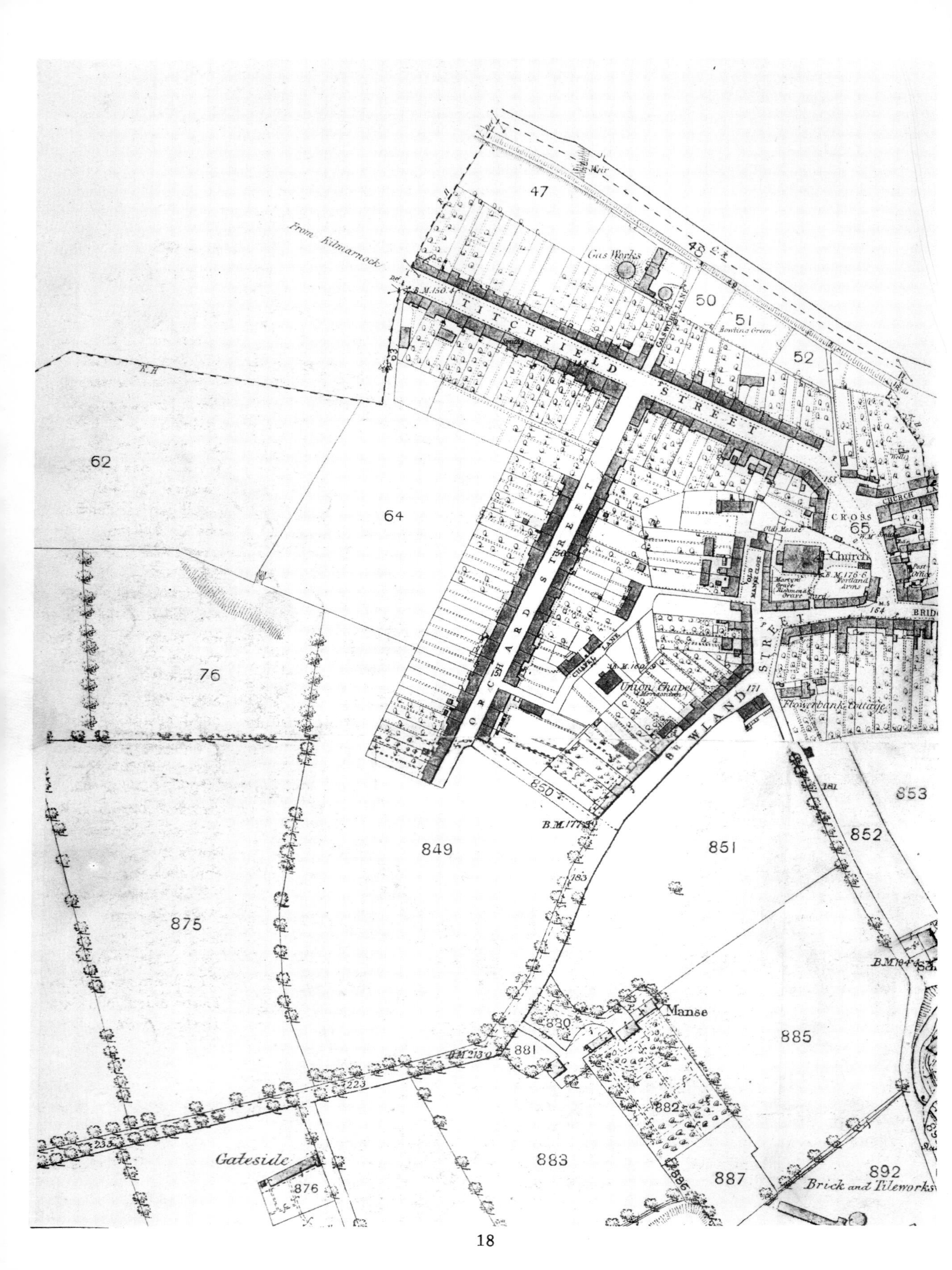
From Kilmarnock
Gas Works
Gasworks Lane
Bowling Green
Titchfield Street
Orchard Street
Chapel Lane
Union Chapel
Old Manse
Old Manse Close
Church
Cross
Portland Arms
Post Office
Flowerbank Cottage
Manse
Gateside
Brick and Tileworks
47
48
50
51
52
62
64
65
76
849
850
851
852
853
875
876
880
881
882
883
885
887
892

GALSTON
IN THE 1860's

This map displays the extent of the town in Galston parish just before the formation of the burgh. The west end of Titchfield Street and Standalane farmlands were in Loudoun parish along with a small patch of land at the Muckle Brig. Streetheid Pit and the Gas Works are in operation while brick and tileworks lie behind the reservoir supplying the lade to Richmond's wool mill in Barr Street. Barr Castle Gardens is the site of the High Bowling Green, and across the railway is Ironworks Square described here as Howie's Square. The straight lines of Polwarth Street, Henrietta Street, Titchfield Street and Orchard Street distinguish them as 19th century additions to the older town close to the church.

BARR MILL

Barr Mill as it was at the end of last century. It was one of the oldest in the district, mentioned in the parish records in 1569 when John Pearson, younger, registered the baptism of his daughter Nancy. It probably belonged to the Lockharts of Barr whose tenants were thirled to it, being required to have their corn ground at that mill only. It is now a ruin although the adjacent miller's house is still occupied. Barrmill was for a while in the hands of the Hunter family one of whom was an acquaintance of Burns, and whose great-grandfather was the discomfited hero of the old ballad "I had a horse I had nae mair." Latterly it belonged to the Steel family. When the 1920 flood swept the milldam away the mill was later powered by a gas engine.

STRATH MILL

Until its demolition after the 1st World War the old paper mill, lying between Newmilns and Galston, was a place of great antiquity. It is mentioned in 1774 in connection with paper-making although earlier records trace it back to 1639. Before production ceased older members of the community remember helping to throw waste-paper into the pulp-grinder. The mill had survived long enough to make cards for the jacquard machines in the lace industry. The lade ran from the dam at Masons Holm, first to Strath and then to Barr Mill. When this photograph was taken in the 1890's the two mill wheels on the premises had been removed, the machinery being worked by a steam engine. Of the group of buildings only Strath Mill Cottage on the left remains and another cottage at the rear.

HAG BRIG

"Do ye mind the Hag Brig turn,
Whaur we guddled in the burn."

The brig is mentioned in the Reverend George Lawrie's nostalgic song, "Lang, Lang Syne," as a place where children played in summer. It also served as a turning point for walkers to and from Newmilns, and was the location where Lord Donington built his barricades to prevent the Newmilns handloom weavers using the Lime Road as a right-of-way in the 1870's and 80's. The bridge took its name from the farm of Hag which once lay between the road and the river. Not so popular as a rendezvous today, it is no longer a place of sylvan beauty, and the old single-carriageway brig is buried under a wide modern road.

AT THE FOUR CORNERS

At the four corners looking from Henrietta Street to the Portland Corner. The left side of the street is similar in appearance today, having avoided the unsightly gaps created in other areas of the town. At the corner is the shop of licensed grocer Alexander Harvey, one of seventeen licensed premises which could be seen from the Four Corners. At the far end of the range of shops by the bridge is Stepends Inn, while above the houses at the entrance to Brewland Street, can be seen the cranes used at the building of the new, central premises of the Co-operative Society, dating the photograph at 1900.

STANDING ORDERS

ENACTED BY THE

COMMISSIONERS OF POLICE

OF THE

BURGH OF GALSTON,

10th June, 1867.

GALSTON:
JAMES TORRANCE, 9 BRIDGE STREET.
1867.

I.—MEETINGS.

In addition to the Statutory Meetings of the Commissioners to be held upon the First Monday after the Annual Election, and and the Second Monday of January, April, July, and October. Special Meetings shall be held on the Second Monday of every other Month at 7 o'clock P.M.. at which hour the Statutory Meetings, with the exception of the first, shall also be held.

In the circulars calling the meetings, all notices of motions shall be inserted, and also a note of the other business to be brought before the meeting as far as practicable.

II.—COMMITTEES.

1.—At the first Meeting of Commissioners after the Annual Election, the following Committees shall be appointed for the year then current viz : (1) a Committee, consisting of three Members, to carry out the purposes the Act as regards Sewerage andC leansing, to be called the "Sewerage & Cleansing Committee": (2) a Committee, consisting of three Members, to carry out the purposes of the Act as regards the Paving and Maintaining and Improving Streets, to be called the "Paving and Streets Committee" : (3) a Committee, consisting of three Members, to carry out the purposes of the Act as regards the supply of Water and Lighting the Streets, to be called the "Water and Lighting Committee". If practicable one of the Magistrates shall be on each committee, and shall be Convener.

2.—No Committee shall have power to Authorise an expenditure of more than £1 without the sanction of the Commissioners.

III.—ORDER OF BUSINESS.

1.—The minutes of the previous meeting shall be read, and, if correct, certified by the signature of the Preses.

2.—Letters, Memorials, Petitions, &c., shall then be read, and, if practicable, disposed of.

3.—Questions may then be asked by Members of the Board, and notices of motions given.

4.—The minutes of Committees shall next be read, and business arising therefrom disposed of.

5.—The motions of which notices have been previously given shall then be taken up in the order in which they stand in the minutes of the Board, and no motion shall be withdrawn without the unanimous consent of the Commissioners present.

6.—Accounts lodged with the Treasurer against the Board shall then be submitted to the meeting, and certified if correct.

IV.—ORDER OF SPEAKING.

No Commissioners shall be allowed to speak more than once on the same question, unless permission be given to explain, or the attention of the Preses be called to a point of order, excepting the mover of a resolution, who shall have right to reply.

V.—MOTIONS.

No motion shall be discussed or adopted at any meeting without notice of it having been given at a previous meeting, unless with consent of Two-thirds of the whole Commissioners.

THE POLICE BURGH

In 1864 Galston became a Police Burgh and very quickly got into its stride as a busy and efficient organisation with a businesslike approach to its problems. These pages show the Standing Orders of the Council, dating from 1867. An interesting comment on the devaluation of the currency since then can be inferred from Section II Note 2, where expenditure without sanction is limited to £1. Another estimable order given under Section IV says, "No Commissioners shall be allowed to speak more than once on the same question".

VIEW FROM THE NORTH-EAST

The Parish Church, on its elevated position in the middle of the town, dominates the scene. This view from the 1890's, looking over the roofs of the old town, is from the northern end of the Muckle Brig. The Burnawn flows into the Irvine at the left hand corner. The two old thatched houses on the south bank are long gone, replaced by the newer houses in Church Lane and the buildings of Sharp's hosiery.

THE RIVER BANK

This view is looking east along the river towards Molmont Hill. On the right is the Loudoun Working Men's Bowling Club. Further upstream the earliest bowling green was situated at the foot of Bowling Green Lane and also the quoiting pitch. Downstream was Riverside Park football field. With all these sporting activities, added to the anglers by the river, this was for a time, the recreational area of Galston.

BRIDGE STREET

Bridge Street in the 1890's. The north side of the street from the Four Corners to the bridge over the Burnawn, had the benefit of four public houses in a row. At the corner in doubtful company, sharing a building with the Commercial Tavern was Mrs. Kerr, milliner. They are followed in sequence by the Crown Hotel, the George Inn and the Black Bull (now the Tudor Inn). A brewer's dray stands in the street, delivering barelled and bottled beer, possibly from Catrine Brewery. At the time, not unlike many mining communities, Galston was noted for its large number of licenses, with a thriving carry-out trade of ale in jugs and tinnies.

VIEW INTO HENRIETTA STREET

From Burnawn Bridge early this century. On the left is the Black Bull Hotel and on the right Stepends Inn, also known as the Bridge Inn. At both sides by the bridge a lane ran along the bank of the Burnawn, giving access to a labyrinth of houses, stables and workshops, including a bakery and a smiddy. At the far end is the entrance to Henrietta Street, named after Miss Scott of Cessnock. The houses at the foot of the hill were built early in the 19th century. At the top can be seen the surface buildings of Streetheid Pit, one of the many coalmines at the verge of the town.

GREAT CHANGES

Great changes in Henrietta Street have taken place since this photograph was taken in the 1890's. From the Four Corners to the top of the street few of the houses seen here remain. One notable exception is the Masons Arms, the two storey building on the left. In 1919 and 1921, a number of houses in the street and in Kilknowe suffered from subsidence in the mine galleries below. Subsidence also occurred in the Glebe in 1922 over the mine workings of the Gauchalland Coal Company, although no coal it was claimed had been brought out in that area since 1907. The pits, once on the periphery, had been overtaken by the expanding town.

CROSS STREET

No great change can be seen at the Cross since this photograph was taken at the beginning of this century. On the right at the end of Titchfield Street was Pat Graham's chip shop, and on the left Muir's, general outfitter. Beyond it is a building dating from 1787, later the parish office, but originally a Sunday School, established by Miss Scott of Cessnock. On the far side of Church Lane was Russell, fruiterer, later the Queen Mary Cafe. The chief alteration lies in the building next to Leslie's shoe shop. It was replaced by the Municipal Chambers in 1926, and had previously housed, upstairs, the town's offices, and downstairs the Portland stables, which were generally used by farming families attending church functions and Sunday services.

Abstract of the Accounts of the Burgh of Galston.

FOR YEAR ENDING 15th MAY, 1886.

I.—*POLICE ASSESSMENT.*

CHARGE.	£	s.	d.
Amount of Police Assessment,...	£159	4	0
Arrears at 15th May, 1885, ...	5	4	7½
Grant from Road Trustees, ...	10	0	0
Burgh Customs, ...	4	18	3
Fines from Police Court, ...	15	9	9½
Rent from Slaughter House, ...	34	5	0
Rent for Bleaching Green, ...	1	18	6
Balance in favour of Treasurer, ...	105	2	7¼
	£336	2	9¼

DISCHARGE.	£	s.	d.
Balance in favour of Treasurer from last Account,	£90	11	10¾
Cleaning Streets,...	34	11	9
Expenses of Police Court, ...	18	18	6
Rent of Board Room, Gas, and Coal, ...	1	0	0
Maintaining Wells, ...	29	13	11½
Salaries, Commissions, &c., ...	32	17	11
Printing, Stationery, &c., ...	6	15	2
Rent for Fire Engine, ...	2	0	0
Lighting Streets, Gasfitting, Wages, &c., ...	42	1	11
Interest on Bank Account, ...	5	0	9
Slaughter House, Interest on Bond, Public Burdens, and Repairs,...	29	2	5½
Disbursements for Carting Gravel, Ashes, &c., Repairs of Streets, ...	10	11	11
Election Expenses, ...	5	8	2
Rent of Bleaching Green and Fencing, ...	3	0	1½
Annual Allowance for Ringing Bell, ...	8	0	0
Assessments relieved, ...	4	12	6
Arrears outstanding, ...	7	2	4
Miscellaneous, ...	4	13	5
	£336	2	9¼

II.—*SEWER ASSESSMENT.*

CHARGE.	£	s.	d.
Amount of Assessment, ...	£28	19	10
Balance in favour of Treasurer, ...	17	2	3½
	£46	2	1½

DISCHARGE.	£	s.	d.
Balance in favour of Treasurer from last Account,	£16	7	7½
Expense of Sewers, ...	11	9	10
Scavenger's Wages, ...	13	5	0
Miscellaneous, ...	4	19	8
	£46	2	1½

III.—*SANITARY ASSESSMENT.*

CHARGE.	£	s.	d.
Balance against Treasurer from last Account, ...	£49	11	5
Half of Feu-duty in Hospital refunded, ...	0	12	6
	50	3	11

DISCHARGE.	£	s.	d.
Maintenance of Hospital, ...	£2	1	2
Inspector's Salary, ...	8	10	0
Burials, ...	1	12	0
Feu-duty, ...	1	5	0
Miscellaneous, ...	2	12	8
Balance against Treasurer, ...	34	3	1
	£50	3	11

IV.—*SPECIAL SEWER ASSESSMENT.*

CHARGE.	£	s.	d.
Subscription from Duke of Portland, ...	£50	0	0
Amount of Assessment, ...	55	10	6
Balance in favour of Treasurer, ...	12	1	10
	£117	12	4

DISCHARGE.	£	s.	d.
Balance in favour of Treasurer from last Account,...	£2	8	10
Interest on Bond, ...	32	6	8
J. & W. Osborne—Balance of Contract, ...	30	9	0
Engineer's Commission, ...	43	15	0
Collector's Commission,...	4	15	6
Miscellaneous, ...	3	17	4
	£117	12	4

ROBERT BLAIR, *Clerk.*
MATTHEW ROBERTSON, *Treasurer.*

THE BENEFITS OF ECONOMY

By 1886 the burgh of Galston was run on the princely sum of five hundred and fifty pounds, one shilling and a penny three farthings. From the abstract of accounts for that year some interesting figures appear. The police court functioned at a loss. Fines brought in over £15, but expenses were just under £19. Burgh customs raised only £4.18s.3d., not enough to cover election expenses, while the largest outlays were in cleaning and lighting the streets, and maintaining wells. No expenditure was required for payments or expenses in the days of amateur councillors, as the largest claim could only have been for shoe leather for the walk from home to the council chamber.

TRINITY CHURCH

Trinity Church was built in Glebeknowes field, behind Glebe School in 1887-88. An atrractive building on its prominent site, it replaced the old Free Church which was built in 1843 at Kilknowe. In 1949 its members joined those of the Erskine Church to form the New Parish Church. Prohibitive costs were necessary for its repair and it was abandoned and demolished in 1963. The joint congregation moved back to the Erskine Church, until all combined with the Parish Church in 1980.

BURNHOUSE

Burnhouse was for long the property of the Cessnock Estate, forming a small village of its own outside the town. The houses were occupied by estate workers and the other buildings included a sawmill, storehouse and barns. Parts of the mill lade can still be seen behind the house on the right where a small outbuilding carries the date 1759. The sawmill in the centre, in this picture from the 1890's, no longer exists, but the rest of the houses are still standing in a pleasant residential area, on the right of the road to Cessnock. In the field on the right of the road between Burnhouse and Cessnock lay the Galston golf course, replaced in 1909 by the new course at Loudoun.

THE DUKE'S YAIRD

The patch of land in the foreground has been used by various firms over the years. Originally, in the possession of the Duke of Portland and a workplace for his employees, it has since been tenanted by Cunningham the cartwright; the County Council roads department; Andrew Kyle, mineral borers; and many others before the present occupants. For a while the slaughterhouse was located there, and in the early days of mechanised transport the heavy Fodens wagons, which collected milk from the farms, were garaged in the yard. The view is from the railway, looking down Barr Street in the 1890's with the old wool mill on the left and behind it the Glebe School, also known as Burnside School. Beside Richmond Bridge is the mill managers house, and next to it, on the right, the only two-storey house in Garden Street, known as the Big Laun, since demolished.

CONGREGATIONAL CHURCH

Members of this church in Chapel Lane were, in the complicated history of the Church of Scotland, seceeders from the United Secession Church, (the Erskine Church). The breakaway occurred in 1843 and the congregation survived as one of the smaller reformed churches in Galston as part of the Evangelical Union. The final meeting of the kirk session was held in October 1962, and the church was pulled down soon after for the housing development in the area.

LOUDOUN LODGE

In its woodland setting between Woodhead Farm and East Newton. It was long known as Symington's from the family which lived there at the time of this photograph at the end of last century. The well-maintained building and garden were features of property on the Loudoun estate, until the heavy estate and legacy duties had their effect on inherited wealth and property this century.

A COUNTRY LASS

The working woman is not a new concept. The life of the people in town and country until recent times was generally hard and physically strenuous. Women were not excluded, being involved most of the day in heavy household tasks, like this Galston woman, barefoot, carrying water from the well.

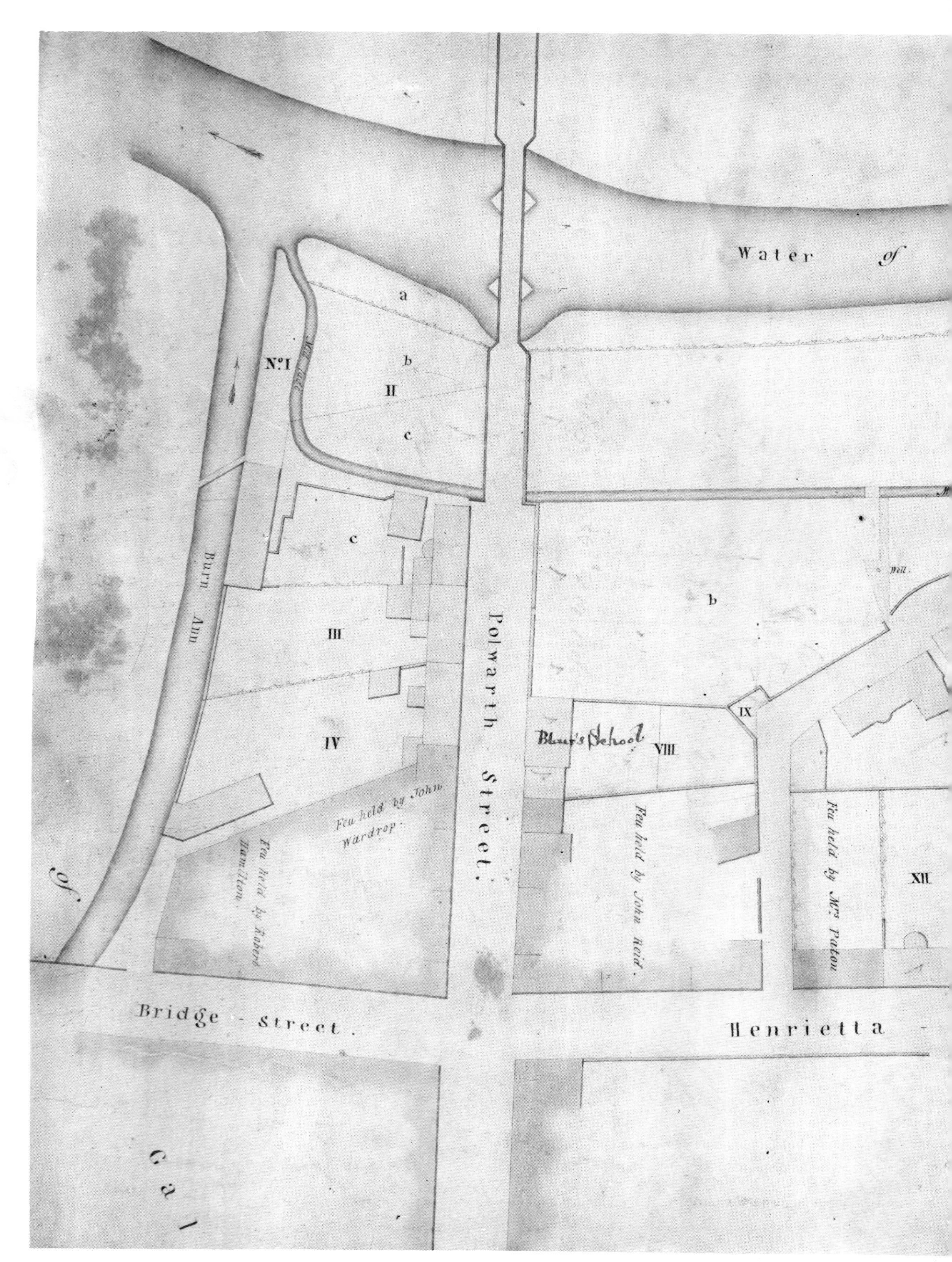

Water of
a
b
c
No. I
II
Mill Lade
c
Burn Ann
III
IV
Polwarth Street.
b
Well
IX
Blair's School
VIII
Feu held by John Wardrop.
Feu held by Robert Hamilton.
Feu held by John Reid.
Feu held by Mrs Paton
XII
of
Bridge - Street.
Henrietta
Gal

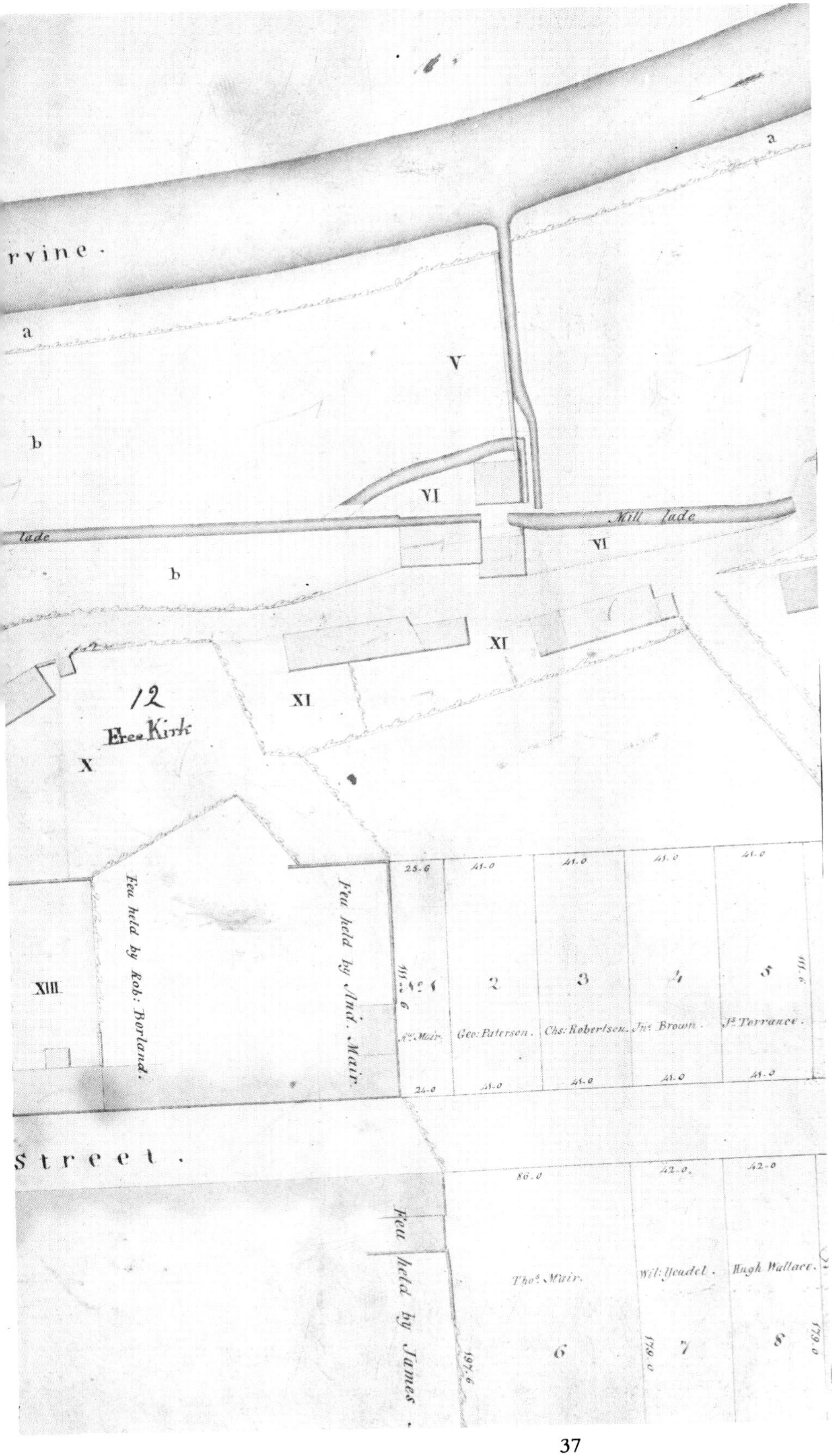

THE LANDS OF LONGHOUSE

The Lands of Longhouse planned in 1837, belonging to the Trustees of the Blair Educational Trust. The shaded areas are of existing buildings in Bridge Street, Polwarth Street, Henrietta Street and Barrmill Road. Other areas are marked as feus given out to local residents. The site of Blair's School and the Free Kirk have been written in. In 1837 only half of Henrietta Street had been built and at Vb a large area of orchards and gardens lay between Barrmill Road and the river, west of the Kilknowe flax and saw mills marked V1. The mill lade runs all the way to the mouth of the Burnawn at 11, where Brown's Institute was later built.

BURNHOUSE COTTAGES

Burnhouse cottages stood opposite Cemetery Road, between the entrance to Sorn Place and Clockston Road. They housed the families of Cessnock estate workers some of whom are pictured here at the turn of the century, during a break from harvesting. The horse is harnessed to a farm cart called a slipe. The pulley and roller apparatus behind the horse pulled the hay or corn rucks on to the cart to carry them to the stackyard. The slipe was also a favourite form of conveyance for children helping at the harvest. Unlike the houses at Burnhouse these cottages did not survive. They were pulled down after the 2nd World War.

THE INN

The Inn at Sornhill seen here in the 1890's on the left of the road from Galston to Sorn, with a woman at the door and a thirsty traveller's pony and trap standing by. Other cottages on the left remain, but those on the right are long gone as fewer houses were required in the countryside as the rural population declined this century. A few years ago a small group of bungalows was built in the field on the left as more people took advantage of the peace of the countryside and in this case an excellent outlook over the Valley.

VILLAGE IN DECLINE

Another view of Sornhill, looking north towards Galston. By the end of the 19th century the cottages on the left were being abandoned until all were gone. What had once been a busy road for horse-drawn traffic grew quiet as a route through to Sorn, Catrine, Auchinleck, Cumnock and places further south. Very soon trade was insufficient to keep open the inn on the far right. The number of families in the village at one time more than twenty was reduced to half a dozen.

AN IDYLLIC SCENE

An idyllic scene and one of few remaining clutches of old cottages are these at Quarryhouse on the Cessnock estate, seen resplendent in their thatch at the end of last century. The road still bends down past them to the Burnawn Bridge behind Cessnock Castle. If piped water and electricity had been led in to more of these country cottages between the two world wars when many were being condemned, more would have survived to enhance the countryside.

THE VILLAGE

The village at Loudoun Kirk took its name from the nearby parish church of Loudoun. It stood in its entirety into the 1930's and was a popular subject with artists and photographers. The view chosen here is from the 1920's and shows how well the cottages were maintained by the householders, and the thatched roofs by the Loudoun estate. Originally occupied by the estate workers; gardeners, foresters, gamekeepers and farm labourers, they later housed the families of the miners in the Loudoun pits. The last cottage which stood near the church gates, tenanted by the beadle, was abandoned at the end of the 2nd World War. One of the houses with garden at Loudoun Kirk had an annual feu duty of three shillings and fourpence and two fat hens.

A PLACE IN THE COUNTRY

A place in the country, sought after by so many today was an ordinary possession for all classes up until the end of the 2nd World War. After that, mechanisation led to the last movement of workers from the land, leaving farms mostly as a family business. The closure of Galston pits also saw the beginning of the end for the miners' rows. The condition of the houses in these places depended on the pride of the tenants, but also on the degree of concern and the economic circumstances of the landlord. The decay of Loudoun Kirk, seen here at its best in the 1920's, coincided with the death of the last Earl of Loudoun and the burden of death duties on the estate.

AN ENCAMPMENT

A fine selection of the homes of travelling people is seen in this picture from the 1890's in a strip of woodland near Loudoun Kirk. Certain sites were visited every year in season, usually at the time of the harvest of grain and root crops, but also in the spring. The people of the road were met with greater tolerance then, as much of their work was acceptable to the public in labouring on the land, and from the sale of useful goods, the result of coppicing in the woods, and the repair of household articles.

ALTON

Until a few years before the 2nd World War there had been a clachan at the Alton for hundreds of years. In the 1890's, it still had a school, and John Nisbet the blacksmith and Jimmie Shields, seen here at his joiner's shop, provided a service for the tenant farmers of Loudoun, while other occupants worked on the estate. At one time up to a dozen families lived in the row of thatched cottages or in others nearby. Each family had a cow and common grazing on the 40 acre park below the village. In earlier days the children had a holiday from the school to help when the cattle went to grass after a long winter. This was known as "The Lifting," when the animals had virtually to be raised in their stalls and supported all the way to the field.

EAST THREEPWOOD

East Threepwood was the home of James Smith the Covenanter, who was shot at Bank on the side of the Burnawn by Captain Inglis's dragoons. Inglis had his quarters at Newmilns Keep with the duty of harassing and penalising the Covenanting population of the district. The photograph shows the small farm in 1902, of which only the lower courses remain, after it was accidentally burned down during the 1st World War. The monument to James Smith, which was built into the wall of the steading can no longer be traced.

A FARMING FAMILY

A farming family at Little Maxwood in the 1890's. The unusual headgear of the farmer, with the child in the box-cart, might indicate that he was off to collect a load from the town or the mill. The farmwife's bare feet was part of the normal style of work in summer around the farm or at the well. The little farms are still disappearing, but until recent times there was a land hunger among the people of the Valley with its rural traditions. This was last satisfied in the provision of small holdings on the Duke of Portland's estate in the 1920's. Fourteen plots of 1½ to 50 acres were given to ex-servicemen of the 1st World War when the large farm of Meikle Maxwood was broken up.

AT BANKHEAD

A small group of cottages was clustered around the mill at Bankhead which had been, at the end of the 18th and beginning of the 19th centuries, a lintmill with associated bleachfields.In this photograph from the turn of the century it is evident how trig and respectable the old cottages could be, a suitable background to a mother and daughter standing by the front gate. Without a gas supply, or later electricity, and sometimes without piped water, the outlying rows and cottages were slowly deserted. The families of miners or agricultural workers who still lived in the country cottages around the town were finally rehoused before the 2nd World War in the County Council scheme in Galston.

WEE LADYTON

It is becoming more difficult to trace the foundations of the large number of cottars' houses which once were scattered throughout Galston and Loudoun parishes. A change in the agricultural economy last century, leading to larger farming units, and increased mechanisation this century, witnessed the disappearance of the small tenant or cottar. He kept a cow and some poultry, and had additional work on the large farms or estates, or possibly in handloom weaving. This picture from the end of last century shows a typical example in Wee Ladyton of a cottar's thatched cottage, stack-yard and garden. It was last occupied before the 2nd World War, but now only the slightest vestiges remain on the land of Gateside Farm.

HAYMAKING

The interest of this photograph taken late last century lies in the number in the band of workers, and the location of the hayfield close to the castle. Every year the Loudoun estate parks were let by auction and local farmers were able to add to their acreage with a successful bid. The area under hay shown here is now heavily overgrown, but was put to good use almost up to the castle walls. The women are wearing drugget aprons and have their heads covered to spend a long day turning hay in the sun. The farmer, fourth from the right, has six women in his band, and three boys.

THE BIG MILL

The big mill visited all the farms in the district. This scene in the 1890's is at Meikle Maxwood farm when the hay threshing took place in August. Hay seed was a valuable crop for sale and for the following year's sowing, while the straw was stacked for winter fodder. Over a dozen workers would normally be required, mostly male, for this strenuous and speedy operation. This was one of the occasions in the farming year when farmers helped each other, at harvest and threshing time, when many hands made light work.

COUNTRY COTTAGES

Isolated or in rows dotted the countryside until recent times. There were rows of houses at Alton, Loudoun Kirk, Bankhead and Hallrigs near the town in Loudoun parish, and at Sornhill, for agricultural workers. These were thatched and had clay or flagstoned floors. Some had lofts with tiny windows or had "blin' attics" without windows. The cottages seen here in the 1890's were on the right of the road at Sornhill, leaving Galston. They disappeared early this century.

CATERERS

Purveys were available for all kinds of social occasions early this century. A large number of bakery firms from the three towns were in competition for everything from house parties to high society weddings. James Loudoun was for a period one of the leaders in the field, sometimes out manoevring his rivals in Galston and Darvel. He is seen here with his vanman and staff of pretty lady assistants, having successfully bid for the catering at an event in Loudoun Castle.

COUNTRY MAIDS

The rural population involved in agriculture in 1891 in the parish of Galston was still well over a thousand. Farm workers formed a large proportion of the population living-in at the farm houses in the case of single females, or in bothies and cot-houses if single or married males. Apart from visits by the steam traction-engine, the work was all done by horse power or by hand. Many of those workers were dairy maids, one of whom is seen here with her milking stool and wooden luggie, looking especially neat for the photographer.

THE HIGHER GRADE SCHOOL

The Higher Grade school was built in Glebe Road in 1910 to extend secondary education in the town and district. New schools were erected and maintained by the parish school boards, replacing the schools of the Established and Free Churches after the Education (Scotland) Act of 1872, and any other endowed schools willing to join the public school system. The photograph was taken near the end of an era of building with stone, and a number of stonemasons are seen here with representatives of the other building trades, foremen and labourers.

BUILDING SQUAD

By mid 20th century the traditional methods of building had practically died out, mostly with the replacement of stonework on the outer walls with bricks and harling. In this view from the 1900's a typical group of masons and joiners is seen in front of a fine piece of construction work in Galston. An area for dressing sandstone is on the left foreground, while the bricks were used on internal partitions. A labourer with his hod stands on the left, and the foreman, who looks like a man with whom few would disagree, is fourth from the right.

HAND DARNERS

This view is of the interior of the grey room of the lace and madras factory of J.M. Robertson, early this century. The women standing on the left are inspecting the cloth as it is drawn over the tables. Faults are repaired by the hand darners seated in front, who are working on madras and tapestry fabrics. The mass production of lace, madras and other textile furnishings from 1880 until after the 2nd World War provided more than enough work for women in the district. Many from Galston travelled to Newmilns and Darvel as only two lace mills opened in the town, in Barrmill Road, J.M. Robertson & Co. (1880), and Peden, Young & Reid (1881), later Hendrie & Co. Neither survived the depression in the trade in the 1960's. Another small lace factory, Yeudall's, was built in Standalane Street in 1920, but it did not re-open after the War.

AYRSHIRE
WHITE NEEDLEWORK

Galston was once a centre for the production of cut muslin or Ayrshhre white needlework. The fine muslin and gauze woven on local handlooms were the raw material for beautiful lace insertions and embroidery. Garments of these were made by women in their own homes to add to the family income. The trade developed in the late 18th century and soon employed hundreds. When fashion changed to heavier materials in Victorian times, the business died away until only christening robes, like the one shown here, and lace caps were made.

SHARP'S

Apart from the blanket Mill, the only survivors of the traditional textile trades of the town were the hosieries, the descendents of the stocking makers. These businesses often developed into knitwear factories capable of a wide variety of knitted goods. In the "Irvine Valley Almanack" for 1881, three stocking framers are listed. One is Mrs William Sharp of Barr Street. The photograph shows part of Sharp's knitwear factory early this century. Situated in Church Lane beside the river it now operates under new ownership as the last representative of the trade.

RAILWAY ENGINES

Glasgow and South-Western Railway Co. engines on the Valley branch line in the 1890's. Both were designed by sons of the Rev. Robert Stirling of Galston. R.5 below was built at Kilmarnock in 1862/63 to the design of Patrick Stirling locomotive superintendent of the company from 1853 to 1866, when he left to become chief locomotive engineer of the Great Northern Railway. He was succeeded by his youngest brother, James Stirling, who designed No. 197 above, built in 1871. James moved on in 1878 to become locomotive superintendent with the South Eastern Railway. Two other brothers, William and Robert of this remarkable family were engineers in Peru. The Rev. Robert Stirling, parish minister, (1824-78) set the family tradition with the invention of the Stirling engine.

RAILWAY WORKERS

Railway workers at the station before the 1st World War, still in the livery of the Glasgow & South Western Railway. The company was formed in 1850 and continued to operate until 1923 when it was absorbed in the London, Midland & Scottish Railway. For almost a century it was the main artery of trade for local industry, and provided permanent employment for a considerable number at all three Valley stations, goods yards and associated signal boxes.

WINTER SPORTS

Old folk say that in former times the winters were colder and the summers sunnier, and it is true that the river Irvine is seldom frozen over as it is in this print from the 1890's. Boys are seen sliding on an icy area near Barrmill between the lade and the river. On the left background behind the railway signal box are the winding gear and surface buildings of Maxwood Pit. Nearby were the Maxwood Rows, two rows of miners' houses. In 1913 single apartments there had a rent of one shilling and seven pence per week, and two apartments two shillings and sixpence halfpenny per week inclusive of rates. There were four water closets for twenty families, no wash houses and only one well.

THE ROARIN' GAME

All three towns in the Valley had curling rinks. Galston's was at Haymouth Loch on the road to Sorn. The picture shows four rinks cleared for play with a game in progress between the home team and Larkhall in February 1893. Behind is Haymouth with the walls of Cessnock gardens. The curling stones were stored in a shed at the corner of the field, but the outdoor game depended on spells of frosty weather, and the sport languished in the first half of this century, up until the construction of indoor rinks.

THE FIRST MOTOR CAR

The first motor car in the Valley belonged to J.H. Turner of Cessnock Castle, factor to the Duke of Portland. He is seen here at the beginning of the century returning with his daughter from an expedition to Kilmarnock. By this time a footman was no longer required to run with a red flag before a motor vehicle. By an Act of 1903 penalties were introduced for reckless driving, although speeds up to 20 m.p.h. were allowed on public highways.

MODERN TRANSPORT

Early in the century the carriage and pony and trap were replaced by horseless carriages. They caused much excitement when delivering house-guests to the castles and mansion houses in the Valley. One is seen here en route to Cessnock, but for all their elegance and style they occasionally broke down leaving the passengers to be rescued by the trustworthy horse. The pleasures of motoring among the rich had been firmly established despite the mishaps.

IN TRAINING

The tug-o-war team had its clubroom at Strath Mill. Here they are at practice, outside the papermill buildings, preparing for the summer season of sports round the turn of the century. The chimney and premises of the mill were demolished after the 1st World War ending the life of the oldest manufactory in the district.

TUG-O'-WAR

Tug-o'-War was a very popular sport last century. The Galston team renowned throughout the land in the 1890's with Wm. Miller their coach, strike a very impressive pose in the Macintosh photographic studio at Strath Mill. Money prizes were given for this event at professional meetings, once common throughout South-west Scotland, but now generally confined to the Highlands and the Borders.

THE BAUR AILLEY

The Baur Ailley was the scene of the thrilling game of handball, believed to have begun in the Middle Ages and played only where the large expanse of a castle wall was available. By the time this photograph was taken at the turn of the century, the playing surfaces underfoot and on the wall had been smoothed over with concrete and cement, and the old tree which restricted play cut down. No date can be given for the origin of the game in Galston, at Barr Castle, but, by 1833 John Wright local poet tells us that —

" . . . o'er all sports athletic, nimble, strong,
Was handball pastime, young, mid-aged and old,
As equals mingled, after practice long,
And scarce a neighbouring village was so bold,
As struggle with our own the sovereignty to hold."

HAUN BA'

Every year on Glasgow Fair Saturday, teams competed for the "World Cup," otherwise known as the Galston Handball Challenge Cup. This picture from the 1920's shows a winning team of three with the Cup.

They are, left to right, Robert Graham, Hugh Craig and Mungo Nisbet, famous players in their day. By the 1930's the game was mostly confined to Galston and the "world champions" were players from the town. The 2nd World War sounded the death knell. The sport died out among the young and no longer were the calls peculiar to the game – "haincher," "bin-hauner" or "hauns oot in love," heard in Baur Ailley, although a number of attractive winners' medals are still prized in the community.

THE GOWF PARK

The Gowf Park was in use for centuries, before Loudoun Gowf Club was formed. The game was played by the Loudoun family, their guests and friends. It is first mentioned in this connection with four entries in Galston parish church records for 1773 when three donations of four shillings, and one of six shillings were donated by the "gentlemen golphers of Loudoun" for the relief of the poor. The photograph shows the Countess of Loudoun driving off, with an unorthodox grip, at the opening in 1909. The course has a number of archaeological features fortunately undisturbed in recent years, including the remains of a pre-historic tomb, which forms an additional hazard on the approach to the first green.

THE GENTLE SEX

The gentle sex could take up golf soon after Loudoun Gowf Club was established, without loss of grace or dignity. Following the efforts of the Rational Dress Movement at the end of the 19th century, frills and flounces were rapidly disappearing and games, once a male preserve, could be played by ladies with style and skill. The battlements of the castle can be faintly seen above the trees on the right as two women play their round, soon after the Club opened. That year T. Black & Son, Ironmongers, Galston were offering:-

"Drivers, Mashies, Cleeks, Lofters, Putters, at 2/- to 4/6d. each.
Balls, 5½d. to 2/- each. Try the 'Colonel' a true flyer at 2/- each.
Golf Bags 3/- to 10/6d."

PIGEON FANCIER

The art of breeding and racing pigeons is still a favoured pastime among miners, but in the past competition was keen to a level of fanaticism and pigeon lofts abounded in mining towns. Among the most successful enthusiasts was Tommy Nisbet of Barr Street, seen here early in the century, with a wealth of prizes and trophies won over the years. An all-round sportsman, he was a first class handball player, as well as an expert in the production of handballs.

SCOUT MUSTER

The first troop in the town was formed in 1911 and recruited both boy and girl scouts for a number of years. This photograph shows a smart turnout for a review a year later at Cessnock Castle. The inspection is made by the Duchess of Portland under the eye of the Scout leader Mrs. Turner of Cessnock. A piper and stretcher party add to the importance of the occasion.

ANNUAL CAMP

Before the days of international scout camps, in all corners of the world, the local troop enjoyed expeditions nearer home. The most popular site was at Burnawn, where the girl scouts appear to be in charge of the catering arrangements, assisted by the junior males. The photograph is pre-1914, before the Girl Guides had been established as a separate organisation, segregating the sexes.

BOY SOLDIER

Before the 1st World War all three Valley towns had large squads of volunteers in the army reserve. Here is a young member of the Galston Volunteer Corps from that time, smartly turned out and ready for parade. This type of service was another outlet at a period when the six-day working week was beginning to slacken its grip. With Saturday afternoons off, and a little more money, new forms of relaxation could be indulged. The attractions of the Volunteers were the camps, manoevres and chiefly rifle practice to compete for the coveted marksmen's cup. There is no record of whether the young man here survived the carnage of the 1914-1918 war.

GALSTON HIGHLANDERS

There was a great increase in all kinds of recreational activity at the end of last century, mostly sporting, but some cultural. The town might not have had any higher proportion of people of Highland extraction than any other in the Lowlands, but it joined in the general increase in interest in the music and dance of the Gael. This well-presented group of piper and four young dancers expresses this interest.

THE WEEKLY SUPPLEMENT AND ADVERTISER,

For GALSTON, NEWMILNS, DARVEL, and HURLFORD.

No. 579.---(Twelfth Year.) **FRIDAY, October 9, 1891.** **Price One Halfpenny.**

SPECIAL SHOW

OF

AUTUMN and WINTER NOVELTIES

IN

MILLINERY,

MANTLES,

DRESSES,

AT

W. F. THOMSON'S,

45 KING STREET, KILMARNOCK,

THE FAVOUR OF A VISIT WILL BE ESTEEMED.

WALTER WILSON & CO.,

5 DUKE STREET, KILMARNOCK,

ARE now showing a Great Variety of Seasonable Goods at Prices that are simply unapproachable in nearly every Class of DRAPERY GOODS. For example :—

BLEACHED TWILLED SETS, PILLOW AND BOLSTER SLIPS,..........11½d, 1s 3½d, and 1s 6½d.
BLEACHED TWILLED SHEETS (Full Size),..........1s 11½d, 2s 6½d, to 4s 6d.
(These Prices are for *PAIRS*, not Single Sheets.)
A FEW FULL-SIZED HEAVY TARTAN PLAIDS,..........At 12s 11d ; Worth 19s 6d.
GREY AND FAWN LARGE-SIZED WRAPS,..........At 2s 6½d.
DRESS TARTANS, IN FANCY AND CLAN PATTERNS,..........At 4¾ per Yd.
BLACK CASHMERES,..........At 1s 2½d to 2s 9½d ; VERY SPECIAL, 1s 4½d.
BLACK AND NAVY SERGES,..........From 8¾d.

THE VALUE TO BE HAD IN OUR MILLINERY AND UNDERCLOTHING DEPARTMENTS IS TOO WELL KNOWN TO NEED PRICES TO BE QUOTED.

WALTER WILSON & CO.,

GRAND COLOSSEUM,

5 DUKE STREET, KILMARNOCK.

BENEFITS TO CASH PURCHASERS.

FOR ONE MONTH ONLY.

TO make room for New Goods which are daily [illegible] Cash Purchasers :—

PIANO, Walnut, Iron Frame, Trichord, Check Action, for £18.
PIANETTE, Walnut, slightly used, Iron Frame, Check Action, £10.
PIANO, £60, second-hand, Rosewood, Colland & Collard, only £20.
PIANO, £40, second-hand, Rosewood, Chappell, for £17 10s.
ORGAN, Handsome Case with Mirror, 10 Stops, 4 Sets Reeds, Couplers, &c., only £12 12s.
ORGAN, 16 Stops, 6 Sets Reeds, Couplers, &c., for £20.
ORGAN, 5 Octaves, Walnut Case, for £6 10s.
HARMONIUM, 5 Octaves, Walnut Case, only £5 10s.

Please note that the above offers cannot be repeated, but to all Cash Purchasers from General Stock of Pianos and Organs I will present a Piano or Organ Stool along with Instruction Book free.

Instruments on hire from 10s per month, to became Hirer's own property when full price has been paid in hires.

JAMES KIRKLAND,

34 BANK STREET, KILMARNOCK.

SAINT-RAPHAEL TANNIN WINE.

STRENGTHENING & DIGESTIVE.

This Wine is an invigorating Tonic, *of most delicious taste*, and more efficacious for convalescent and debilitated persons, than iron or quinine.

FOR SALE BY

ROBERT YOUNG, Henrietta Street, GALSTON.

MONUMENTAL WORKS,

HEAD OF JOHN FINNIE STREET, KILMARNOCK,

(Within one minutes walk of the Railway Station)

ANDREW CALDERWOOD,

SCULPTOR.

JACKSON & CO.'S

FOR

Marriage, Birthday, or other Presents.

VARIETY AND VALUE UNEQUALLED.

LARGE STOCK OF

WICKER CHAIRS, TABLES,
FLOWER STANDS,
NEWSPAPER RACKS,
AND
ALL KINDS OF BASKETS,

All Reduced this Month to make room for New Goods.

SPLENDID SELECTION OF

HAIR AND CLOTH BRUSHES,
HOUSEHOLD BRUSHES OF EVERY DESCRIPTION,
DOOR MATS, CHAMOIS SKINS, SPONGES, &c.,

At Lowest Possible Prices.

JACKSON & CO.,

FANCY GOODS WAREHOUSE AND GENERAL STORE,

36 KING STREET,

KILMARNOCK.

NON-INTOXICANT

SPARKLING

"HOP BITTER ALE."

A light refreshing Tonic.

It may be taken constantly at meals, or at any other time with the greatest safety; its regular use tending to promote health, and aid digestion.

Being strictly non-intoxicating, total abstainers will find it a safe, palatable, and refreshing drink; whilst

---

ACCOUNT OF THE INCOME AND EXPENDITURE

OF THE

SCHOOL BOARD of the PARISH of GALSTON,

For Year ending 15th May, 1891.

Dr.	£	s.	d.
To School Fees—Cookery (Evening Classes)	£3	7	11
,, Grants from Scotch Education Department :—			
Annual Grants...	663	13	6
Probate Duty Grant under Minutes of 21st December 1888 and 30th January 1891	406	9	0
,, Amount paid by Rating Authorities at 5d per £, the Rateable Value of the District being £29,830	617	16	6
,, Income from Endowment Galston and Loudoun Educational Trust	110	0	0
,, Income from other sources, viz. :—			
Grant from Galston and Loudoun Educational Trust for Apparatus ...	11	0	0
Rent of Class Room	1	0	0
,, Balance on 15th May 1891 (overdrawn from Bank), on Capital Account ...	690	4	8
	£2503	11	7

Cr.	£	s.	d.
By Balance on 15th May 1890	£238	8	9
,, Expenses incident to the Election of the Board	5	5	2
,, Salaries of Officers of the Board ...	50	0	0
,, Salaries of Teachers	1129	1	0
,, Erection, Enlargement, and Alteration of School Buildings...	692	4	0
,, Printing, Postages, Advertising, and Office Charges, ...	6	6	3
,, Books, Apparatus, and Stationery :—			
For Schools	40	13	2½
,, Rent, Rates, Taxes, and Insurance :—			
For the Board	2	0	0
For Schools	39	4	9
,, Replacement of Furniture and Repairs to Buildings and Furniture :—			
For Schools	27	9	6½
,, Fuel, Fight and Cleaning :—			
For Schools	90	4	6
,, Interest on Loans	48	12	7
,, Repayment of Loans	90	0	0
,, Expenditure, not included above, viz :			
Professional Services (Medical) ...	7	8	0
Taking Census	5	5	0
Interest on Bank Account... ...	31	8	10
	£2503	11	7

Outstanding Liabilities of the Board at 15th May 1891, viz. :—

	£	s.	d.
Balance of Loans sanctioned under Sec. 45 of the Education (Scotland) Act, 1872	£1276	13	4
Other Liabilities, viz. :—Overdrawn from Bank	690	4	8
	£1966	18	0

JAMES CUNNINGHAM, Treasurer of Board.

Examined and found correct,

(Signed) JAMES M. ROBERTSON.
(,,) JOSEPH HOOD.

2nd October, 1891.

SAVE 6D A POUND BY USING

COLVILL & CO.'S

CELEBRATED TEA.

2s PER LB.

A BLEND of the Choicest and Richest TEAS selected with great care.

NOTE—WE HAVE NO FINER.

SPLENDID TEA, 1s 10d per lb. Suitable for Retailers, Hawkers, &c
VERY FINE TEA, 1s 8d per lb. We have a large sale for this Tea.
WONDERFUL TEA, (Specially blended for these dull times), 1s 6d per lb., 4½ per Quarter.

This is not common but really FINE QUALITY TEA. The sale of this Tea has increased enormously of late. It cannot be beat. Sold to all classes, and appreciated by every one.

COFFEES AS ON THE CONTINENT

THE FINEST COFFEE, &c., 1s 6d per lb., 4½d per quarter.
SPLENDID COFFEES, &c., 1s 4d, 1s 2d, and 1s per lb.
EXTRAORDINARY VALUE, 10d per lb., 2½d per quarter.
FINEST PURE COFFEE, 1s 8d per lb., 5d per quarter.

TERMS—CASH WITH ORDER.

OBSERVE THE ADDRESS—

COLVILL & CO.,

WHOLESALE TEA AND COFFEE MERCHANTS,

50 TRONGATE, GLASGOW.

(ESTABLISHED IN 1846.)

DENTISTRY.

MR. DUNLOP, SENR.,

(OF MESSRS. [illegible]

SURGEON DENTISTS, KILMARNOCK),

RESPECTFULLY announces to the Inhabitants of NEW CUMNOCK, MUIRKIRK, AUCHINLECK, &c., that he visits OLD CUMNOCK on the SECOND THURSDAY of each month.

Consulting Rooms—MR. JAMES M'KECHNIE, Pastry Baker, Glaisnock Street. Hours from 1 till 6 p.m.

Consultations daily at No. 1 Portland Road (corner of John Finnie Street.

MARRIAGE INVITATIONS, in Silver or Gold, at prices from 3s. for 25 Invitations, with envelopes to match, at *Supplement* Office.

MITCHELL'S MATCHES.

MITCHELL & CO., GOVAN, GLASGOW.

The Kilmarnock Drapery Warehouse.

JOHN M. GARTSHORE

WILL, ON

FRIDAY AND SATURDAY, 9th and 10th OCTOBER

MAKE A GRAND DISPLAY OF THE LATEST AND MOST FASHIONABLE NOVELTIES THAT HAVE BEEN PRODUCED FOR THE SEASON.

EVERY DEPARTMENT IS FULLY STOCKED WITH GOODS OF THE HIGHEST CLASS CHARACTER, AND OFFERED AT THE LOWEST POSSIBLE PRICES

THE SUPPLEMENT

"The Supplement" or to give it its full title "The Weekly Supplement and Advertiser" for Galston, Newmilns, Darvel and Hurlford was printed by William McDonald and Sons, residing at Rockcliff, Bentinck Terrace, and published by them at their shop in Bridge Street. "The Supplement" started publication in 1880 as the first weekly newspaper in the Valley. It continued without rival until 1908 and the publication in Newmilns of the "Irvine Valley News," which subsequently acquired "The Supplement" in 1923, although it was still issued as a separate sheet until 1945. In 1963 the "Irvine Valley News and Galston Supplement" was bought by the "Kilmarnock Standard" and disappeared from the scene, much lamented, as an independent sheet on Friday 30th December 1966.

THE HUB OF THE TOWN

The hub of the town in the 1920's was still the Four Corners. Hotels, shops and workplaces thronged the area, and before the spread of council housing a large number of the population lived nearby in overcrowded conditions. Motor traffic began to appear in the streets, mostly delivery vans, but children could still play safely as the little girl with her gird is on the right.

BROWN'S INSTITUTE

Brown's Institute stands in Polwarth Street on a small plot of land once partly owned by the Blair's of Longhouse. Behind it may be seen the only part of the Kilknowe mill lade remaining, as it emerges from under the road into the Burnawn. On the corner on the other side of Church Lane was one of the oldest buildings in the street, now demolished, where Mrs. Young had a dish shop. Down the lane her sons had a cycle repair and gramophone shop, before they moved, as Young Bros, to establish their garage in Titchfield Street. Over the bridge on the left is the building which was the Union Bank of Scotland, when this view was photographed in the 1920's.

EDUCATION IN GALSTON

Educational provision goes back centuries in the town. There was a parish school attached to the church in the 17th century. By the early 19th century classes for the children of the free church members were held in the castle. It was called Barr School until the new school of the same name was built in Station Road. A free school for poor children opened in Polwarth Street in 1841 under the terms of Charles Blair's bequest. Later in the century Burnside School was erected to meet the legal requirements of compulsory primary education. Secondary education arrived with the construction of the Higher Grade School seen here in the 1920s from Richmond Bridge.

ENTRANCE TO HISTORY

The oldest doorway in Galston leads into Barr Castle. A memorial stone above recalls two famous visitors, the Reformers, George Wishart and John Knox. Since vacated by the Lockhart family, and not required by the new owners, the Campbells of Cessnock, as a domicile, it has been used as a barn, a grain store, a town jail, a cholera hospital, a school and a religious meeting house. It was acquired from the Duke of Portland by the local Masonic Lodge in 1894 who have maintained it until the present day.

BRIDGE STREET IN THE 1920's

The old established business of R.A. Hutchison, grocer and provision merchant (as mentioned in the "Vale of Irvine Almanack" of 1881) is on the left. It was better known in the 1920's as Charlie Hynds.' Across from it is the shop and printing works of Wm. McDonald & Sons, publishers of "The Weekly Supplement and Advertiser." In the gap in buildings before the "Black Bull Hotel" is the bridge of the Burnawn, from which the street took its name. It was first built in 1640 over the ford which had given access to the houses being built further east.

A TYPICAL VIEW

A typical view of Galston men at leisure, seen here at the door of Browns Institute. It was built in 1874 by Miss Martha Brown of Lanfine at a time when institutes for working men were springing up all over the country to provide facilities for education and recreation. Work was becoming less of an all-day affair (six days a week) as trade unions struggled to improve hours and conditions of work. It would be safe to say that most of the men here, around fifty years ago were miners or ex-miners, who made good use of the Institute up until the 1950's. Thereafter social habits and family traditions changed, and the groups of miners who met at various parts of the town disappeared from the streets, and with them their formative influence on youth.

PAST AND PRESENT

Many of the old houses in Wallace Street had been replaced by the 1920's, and buses had begun to make their difficult negotiations at the Four Corners. On the right and left nearest the camera substantial sandstone shops and houses appeared on the sites of the earlier buildings. Only the Railway Inn has retained its thatch, but even that had gone long before a fire in 1974 led to its rebuilding. It was renamed officially as what it had always been known – The Wee Train.

THE BUTTERCUP

Galston's branch of the Buttercup Dairy Company was in Wallace Street, but there was hardly a small town without one of these little shops excellently fitted-out with easily cleaned tiled surfaces and supplies of fresh dairy products. The company was one of the early examples of the chain store, but specialising in one main line. Jean Parker and her assistant seem pleased with their new window display, promoting margarine. Galston people did not stint themselves of food, so it is doubtful if many switched to margarine at one shilling, even if butter was dear at one shilling and three pence per pound.

WILSON'S STABLES

Wilson's Stables were in the building, still standing, at the corner of Duke Street and Station Road. The largest contractors in the town, their main premises were in Chapel Lane with additional stables near the manse. Their horses and carts were a familiar part of the street scene in the earlier part of this century. Wilsons were undertakers as well as carrying out the normal business of carriers, and some of their workmen had, at times, to make a hurried transition from coalman to pall-bearer. This old established firm never changed to motor transport and was wound-up after the 2nd World War.

"STOURIE AGGIE"

A number of Galston firms were quick to introduce motorised public transport after the 1st World War. There were Brown Bros & Anderson; Forsythe's; Young Bros; Swanson's; and Farrell & Anderson. Many like "Stourie Aggie" had no windows at the sides, and passengers had to brave the elements winter and summer. Here she is standing at Darvel Square in the 1920's, waiting for customers to take the bumpy road to Killie.

THE WAR EFFORT

In the 1st and 2nd World Wars large sums of money had to be raised to pay for armaments. Galston excelled in this work and was able to pay for eight warplanes to which the town's name was attached. The picture is of a biplane F2071 with "Galston No. 6" painted on the fuselage, produced near the end of the 1st World War. During the 2nd World War the drive to encourage war savings took precedence, but all kinds of scrap was collected, iron railings from front garden walls, aluminium pots and pans for the light-weight modern aircraft, and waste paper for reprocessing. Even school children played their part harvesting rose- hips to make rose-hip syrup.

GALSTON'S MEMORIAL

The inaugural service in 1919, at the corner of Duke Street and Station Road, of the memorial to servicemen who died in the 1st World War, was attended by the major part of the town's population. The background is different today. The railway station behind the pillar of the memorial has been replaced by the telephone exchange, and the railway workers houses transformed into modern bungalows. Added to the monument are the names of those lost in the 2nd World War.

A NEW MILL

Handloom weaving had virtually died out by the time the machine-lace industry was introduced in Darvel and Newmilns in the mid 1870's. But in the early 1880's Robertson's and Hendrie's built factories at the east end of the town with up to 30 lace machines between them at the maximum. Lace manufacture was a trade of booms and slumps, and during one of the booms after the 1st World War, Abraham Yeudall built a small factory in Standalane Street to hold three Nottingham lace machines. This is a picture of the first one being installed in 1920.

RIVER IN SPATE

The Lammas Floods were a common occurrence over the years. These were often in the month of August with a sudden rising of the river Irvine after heavy rain. This one which has engulfed a cottage near the bank was on 21st August 1923. The lower part of the town was a regular victim, but in the last fifty years the river seems to have been tamed, by unknown circumstances, and flooding is now a rare event.

THE BAKEHOUSE

Hopkins' bakehouse lies beside the Burnawn and behind the shop in Bridge Street. It has been in the hands of the same family for a century. This picture is from 1929 and Mr. Alex Hopkins is shown third from the right, with his sons Alex and Robert to his left and three apprentices to his right. They have been preparing caps, or cappie biscuits, a favourite item in the miner's piece, and still made on the premises. In the 1930's this firm won a number of gold and silver medals in baking exhibitions in Glasgow and London.

BRANCH PREMISES

Branch premises of the Co-operative Society were opened in Titchfield Street in 1930, beside part of the original buildings of the Society including the bakehouse. It is now closed and with the old buildings at the rear in Gas Lane are redeveloped for private housing. Mr. John Alexander, manager, is shown here with his five assistants on opening day. Along with the private traders at the time, the "Store" gave employment to many local people, retained a large proportion of the townspeople's income within the community, and helped maintain a thriving retail trade.

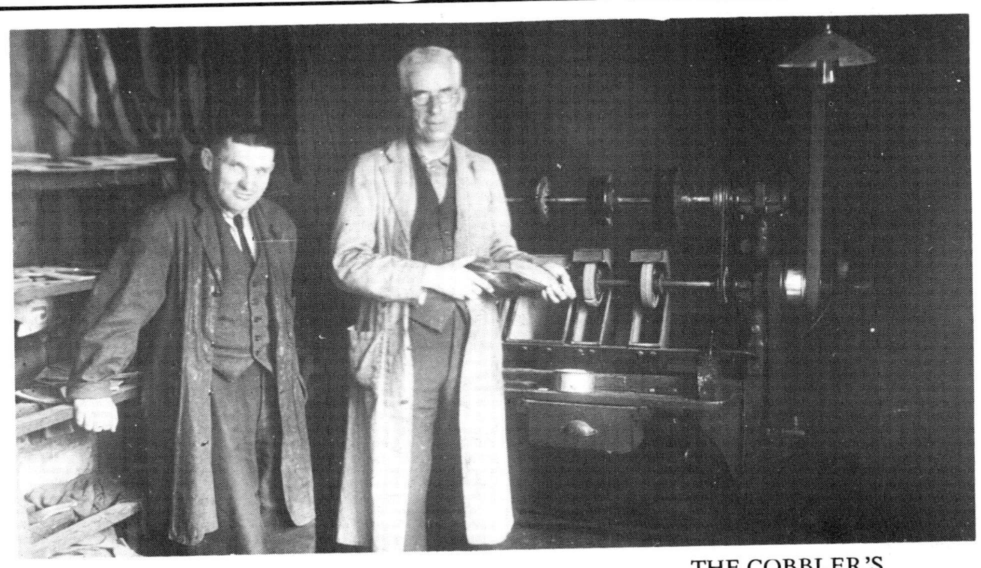

THE COBBLER'S

Tom Adams had his shop at the foot of Henrietta Street. There he made old shoes look like new when leather was the basic raw material and shoes, with care, might last a decade. His "assistant" here is Bennie Connell a famous Galston character who ran messages for a number of Galston citizens. The pace of life was gentler then. People often looked in to chat with tradesmen while they worked. The cobbler, blacksmith, joiner, and others had a number of idle visitors during each day.

SHOE SHOP

In Polwarth Street, still there under new owners was the shoe shop of John Parker, bootmaker whose daughter Lizzie is on the right in this photograph from the 1920's. Small shoe shops, often in association with a cobbler or shoe repair service, have shown remarkable resilience in the face of competition from large stores in the big towns. This was one of the original trades in the town. There were 21 at work in 1791, making shoes for Kilmarnock merchants.

MINE RESCUE

Danger in local pits came from black damp rather than fire damp. The Burnbank and Waterside Rescue Team are pictured here at Loudoun Pit in the 1920's. They were required to be expert in rescue and resuscitation, carried the heavy breathing apparatus of the period, and safety lamps. Small birds were taken along to test for gas, seen here beside the practice dummy on a stretcher.

GALLOWLAW CAIRN

Molmount Hill commemorates the martyrdom of the Covenanter, James Smith of East Threepwood in 1684. The modern cairn was photographed soon after its construction by Galston miners during the General Strike in 1926. It is set on the site of a prehistoric stone circle, destroyed in the late 18th century. From 1926 to 1939 the spot was favoured for picnics and outings by local churches and other organisations and the cairn with its viewing-mirrors, direction finder, wind vane and memorial tablets remained in good condition. Since the War it has slowly deteriorated, despite a few attempts at restoration.

BACK SHIFT

Miners in the 1920's ready to report for work. They carry carbide lamps, the normal means of illumination in Galston pits, as naked lights were generally safe in mines free of fire damp. Danger arose from stey workings near the surface, as at Gauchlland No. 4, where an inrush of liquid and slurry in June 1927 killed two miners. Two others were rescued from the section in the worst accident in a local pit this century.

LOUDOUN PIT

Pictured here in the 1920's are men on their shift underground in Loudoun Pit owned by William Baird & Co. The snap was taken by the pit surveyor with a magnesium flash, giving a rare view of conditions in the roads of a Galston mine. Andrew Holland the youngest of the group stands behind the miner on his hunkers. The major seam in Loudoun No. 3. was 5½ feet thick. Old miners claim the district had the finest coal in Scotland, a hard coal known as stane coal. This pit was closed in 1932 after flooding. Some opencast mining has been carried out recently on both the Galston and Loudoun side of the Valley.

BETWEEN SHIFTS

Between shifts miners passed their time in a number of outdoor activities: football, handball, pigeon fancying, whippet racing and poaching. Another recreation was pitch-and-toss, a mild and illegal form of gambling held in quiet country retreats. It could nevertheless separate an intemperate man from his weekly wage. This group of miners pictured here about 1920 was known as the Red Lion Crowd, who congregated at the foot of Orchard Street. They are heading in the direction of a pitch-and-toss "school" near Loudoun Kirk.

THE SAWMILL

The old mill at Kilknowe was acquired by W. & A. Yeudall and converted into a sawmill, but early this century had begun to prove unsuitable and too constricted. A new yard was opened up further east on Barrmill Road and the photograph shows the interior of the new sawmill building, in the 1930's, with its wood-cutting and dressing machinery, run from an engine powered by burning sawdust. The hardwood timber came from local woodlands and was used in agricultural and mining work as well as building.

AN OUTFITTER'S

An outfitter's for men and women was situated at 4 Polwarth Street. It belonged to Mr. Archie Piper seen here at the door of his shop. On the left is his sister Miss Jean Piper who later carried on the business. For a cloth cap wearing male population in the 1930's there appears to be a good line in bonnets at half-a-crown each, while the window on the right displays a variety of ladies' garments. At a later date the shop also sold white china dishes.

PRENTICE'S HOSIERY

Prentice's Hosiery in Titchfield Street carried on the tradition of the numerous stocking-framers in the town early last century. Prentice's started operating in the 1920's, making all kinds of knitted goods. Among the women workers standing beside the winding machine are Bill and Gary Prentice. The firm closed down recently leaving only one, Sharps, in this line of business. The old houses facing Titchfield Street, once part of the hosiery, have been renovated as dwellings.

COMPETITION

Competition, chiefly from abroad, has led to the contraction of the textile industries in Scotland in recent years. A wide variety of textiles were made in the past in the Irvine Valley, including lace, madras, tapestry, chenille, lappets, carpets, blankets, plaidings, flannels, druggets, winceys and hosiery. After the Second World War around 400 women were still employed in the two Galston lace and madras factories, three hosieries and the blanket mill. In this photograph another group of workers in Prentice's knitwear factory spare a moment for the cameraman.

STRATH DAM

One of the most pleasant walks for old Galstonians was upstream along the south side of the river, with the added attraction of three working mills within a mile of the town. The first was the sawmill at Kilknowe. Next, corn was ground at Barrmill and further along at the old paper mill at Strath Mill the third type of production was made possible by water power from the river. The lade started at Strath Dam, shown here, east of Strath Farm. The great floods of the early 1920's carried most of the dams away on the upper part of the river, and the mills either closed down or installed another source of power.

SHOPS AT THE CROSS

Taken in the 1950's, before the construction of a branch of a supermarket chain, this view is of the buildings between the Burgh Chambers and R.A. Hutchisons. They were occupied by Tom Aitken, plumber, and Sam McVie, hairdresser. Provost White, grocer, had earlier owned the shop on the left, and also had a jam-making factory in what became the Band Hall in Bowling Green Lane. A typical and pleasing feature of Scottish architecture is the pend on the right, leading from the street to yards and workshops in the rear. Many years ago at the annual Cauld Fair an old woman sold candy from its shelter.

SMALL TRADERS

Small traders in Wallace Street in post-war years. Citizens of Galston were renowned for their friendliness to each other and to strangers, most notably in the small shops. Local news was part of the service in the sale of goods. Here at No. 9 was the butcher's shop of Mr. & Mrs. Archie Taylor and at No. 13 was Miss Jenny Morton, home-baker. Standing at No. 11 is Mr. Arthur Smith, for long a familiar figure as an inspector on the bus routes of the Western S.M.T. Company.

THE BUCK'S HEAD TAVERN

The Buck's Head Tavern in Bridge Street in the 1950's. It is shown before the traditional public house frontage was lost in this impressive sandstone building with its carved head over the arched doorway, between the tavern and A.D. Dunn's baker shop and restaurant. Earlier the shop had been the premises of William "Baker" Lee who was talented in making both pastry and poems.

SORN ROAD

Sorn Road looking towards Station Road. On the left the road runs down to Burnhouse, and on the right the Clockston Road is one of the back roads to Newmilns. One of the signatures on the National Covenant of 1638 is James Meikle of Cloksland, but no trace of Clockston can now be found. In the end house of the Burnhouse Cottages, seen here in the 1930's a keen practitioner in the art of topiary once lived, perhaps a gardener at Cessnock. The site of this cottage is still marked by a poor survivor of his work. By the time the 2nd World War opened Galston was already changing rapidly. Old landmarks vanished and the close interaction broke down between the country and the town.

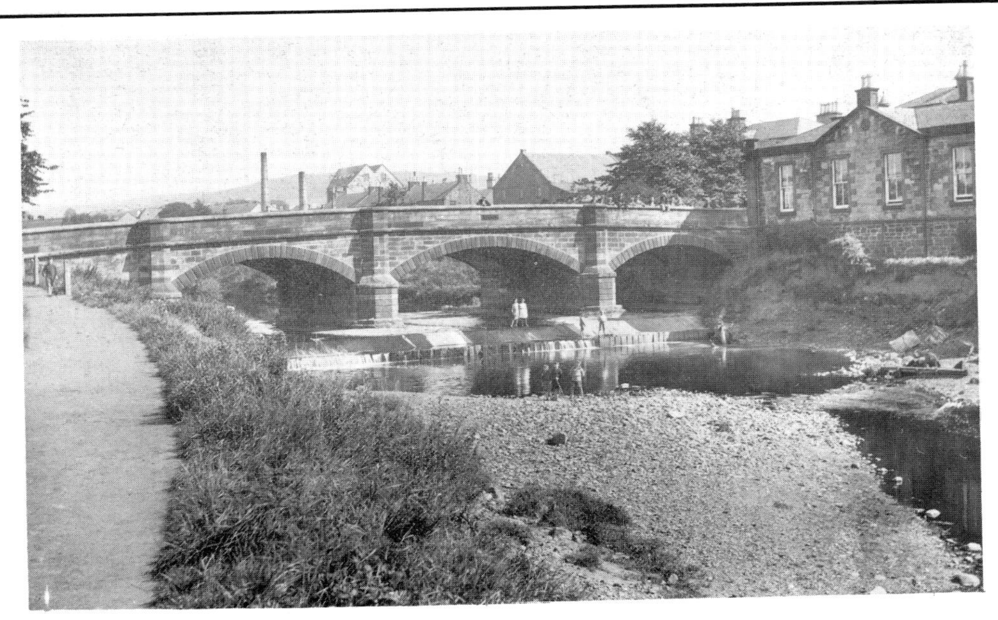

THE MUCKLE BRIG

The Muckle Brig looking upstream, pictured here in the 1930's. It was built in 1839 and opened with great ceremony and commotion, when Captain Patrick, factor at Loudoun, interrupted a fiery radical speech by Hugh Brown, master at Barr School and author of the poem "The Covenanters." Over the bridge from the left are the chimneys of Hendrie & Co., and J.M. Robertson & Co., and then the sombre lines of the old Free Church, built in 1843 and later incorporated in Robertson's lace mill. On the right is Brown's Institute. The bridge is almost 150 years old and is associated with the growth and development of the modern town.

A MUSICAL TRADITION

The Band is shown here in 1924 at the High Bowling Green, after its success as 3rd Class winners over twenty other bands at a contest at Douglas Water. Provost Kyle patron of the Band stands in the centre of the back row, and James Connell, bandmaster for over twenty years is in the centre behind the drum. The Band was formed by the Gauchalland Coal Company as a reed band in 1872, changing a few years later to brass, as Galston Burgh Band. It has now been in continuous existence for over a century, keeping the brass tradition alive, when other more famous outfits fell by the wayside.

HAMILTON'S OF HOLMES

Hamilton's of Holmes were the best-known threshing contractors in the district, providing most of the traction engines and threshing machines to local farms. This print is from the 1920's, but it is typical of the threshing season for a decade or more after the 2nd World War, until the introduction of the combined harvester. Women workers helped at the corn harvest, opening sheaves and carrying away the cauf (chaff). Hamilton's engine "Jeannie" is seen here at Goatfoot farm, with Alex Woodburn, the farmer, the tall figure in the centre of the group. The stacks built in the background are in the traditional Ayrshire style.

THE OLD YEW TREE

The old yew tree at the south front of Loudoun Castle is believed to be over 800 years old. If so, it predates the first stone tower on the site, built in the 15th century, forming the central structure of the modern castle. Yew trees were planted near castles and in churchyards in the Middle Ages to supply the bows of soldiers and huntsmen. The tree itself figures in history. The exiled James, 2nd Earl of Loudoun, addressed secret letters home from Holland to his Countess during Covenanting times thus:— "To the Guidwife at the Aulton, At the Auld Yew Tree Loudoun, Scotland." Tradition also says that Hugh, 3rd Earl, one of the Commissioners for the Treaty of Union, had drawn up drafts of the articles of the treaty, within its shade. This photograph from the 1930's was taken when the castle was still a family home. The yew tree survived the disastrous fire of 1941.

THE BOOLERS

The Boolers of Loudoun Working Men's Club play on a green in Loudoun Parish, on an area of land south of the river once part of Standalane Farm which belonged to the Loudoun estate. Last century houses were built at the west end of Titchfield Street to accommodate mining families. Part of it was also used as a bowling green. This photograph from the 1920's shows a large number of the membership with two of the season's trophies. In the background is the gasometer of the local gas works.

MINING GROUP

Two of the streets at the west end of the town in Loudoun parish were John Street and Boyd Street, named after the coalmasters John and Boyd Gilmour. They were typical of the miners' rows hastily and cheaply constructed last century to house the growing number of miners. This print is from the 1920's when the industry was on the edge of extinction and shows some of the miners who used to meet at one of the street corners. Both streets were replaced after the 2nd World War by the new housing scheme with only the Boyd Street name retained. The three men on the left in the front row are in the characteristic crouching position adopted by miners — on their hunkers!

SENIORS

Galston had a senior football team from 1890 until the beginning of the 2nd World War. The picture is of the Scottish Qualifying Cup team of season 1935/36 which they won in 1936. Earlier they had success in the Ayrshire Cup, winning it in 1903, 1904, 1908, 1913, 1914 and 1925. They also won the Scottish Consolation Cup in 1913. Their games were played at Portland Park and before that at Riverside Park, which proved a great handicap to visiting teams unfamiliar with its hazards.

A WINNING TEAM

The Higher Grade school team won the Kilmarnock and District Schools Cup in 1925. They carried off the trophy in the second year of the competition at Rugby Park, after losing 1-0 to Hurlford in the previous final. All the boys were under the leaving age of fourteen years, but in the period between the two world wars, when the football craze was at its peak, large crowds attended the final stages of the cup-ties in schools football. They welcomed home successful teams with universal enthusiasm in procession behind the band.

THE THREE MUSKETEERS

The three musketeers, or the last of the Galston characters seen at a Gala Day in the 1930's. They are Jimmie Collins, Bennie Connell and Willie Rawson, brother of the equally famous Nellie Rawson. The children are happy to be photographed with these three well-known figures who lived in milder times, when everyone was assured of a place in the community. Galston last century was renowned for its natural wits and eccentrics so well described in the entertaining little book by Robert Young, "Galston Characters."

V.I.P's.

Many celebrated persons have visited the district over the years from the Scottish patriots William Wallace and Robert Bruce, during the Wars of Independence, to Winston Churchill early in the 2nd World War. Unpopular with the miners between the wars, he redeemed himself in their eyes from 1940-45. As Colonel-in-Chief of the Royal Scots Fusiliers he is shown at Loudoun Inspecting the 6th Battalion, and stroking an apprehensive mascot.

LOUDOUN GOWF CLUB

After an early struggle to survive, the Club by 1984 and its 75th anniversary had reached a prosperous period in its history. In the 1960's a new clubhouse had been built, the course purchased and greatly improved. It was a far cry from the days when it was rented and cattle and sheep grazed on it to pay the rent. This view taken in the late 1940's, before the great surge in popularity for the game, shows the old wooden pavillion and the standard kit of wooden shafted clubs and canvas golf bags.

RENOVATION

One of the earliest post-war changes occurred in Barr Street. The area once occupied by the old woollen mill by the Burnawn was levelled and cleaned up. The cottages still standing in this photograph near Barr Castle had reached the end of their life-span and were soon after replaced by council housing. Their new occupants live next to the oldest building in Galston, solid and durable, looking into the future and life in the 21st century.

THE SHOP IN THE SUBURBS

There was a great explosion of council housing before and after the 2nd World War, to rehouse families from the crumbling miners' rows in the countryside and from the older property in the town. Most of the new building occupied the area between the Kilmarnock and Ayr roads to the west. To meet the needs of the area Galston Co-operative Society opened a new shop in Milrig Crescent providing an alternative to a long trek to the town centre.

SWEETIES AND COMICS

There is no mystery about the location of small shops at strategic corners, especially near schools. This one in New Road was a favouite haunt of children on route to the Glebe Road schools, where a daily stock of life-preserving sweets and alternative reading material could be purchased. It was an extension on the property of John Borland, former printer with the "Galston Supplement" and the "Irvine Valley News", and weekly columnist under the pseudonym "Sifter". It was later occupied by John R. Brown before demolition in the late 1960's.

TEMPORARY HOUSING

Temporary housing helped to meet the great demand for accommodation after the War, when traditional building methods could not cope. The prefabricated houses seen here at Castleview Avenue endeared themselves to the families who occupied them. Although of no great architectural merit, they had modern facilities and a scale suitable to a small town setting. Overlooking "Loudoun's Bonnie Woods and Braes," they eventually completed their estimated life-span and were replaced by the tall blocks of flats now occupying the site.

CLERGY IN PROCESSION

Clergy in procession in 1957 at St. Sophia's Church in Bentinck Street. It was built in 1886 under the patronage of the 3rd Marquis of Bute, with a gift in honour of his mother, formerly Lady Sophia Hastings of Loudoun, sister of Lady Flora of tragic memory. The church a scaled down version of Santa Sofia's in Istanbul, serves the Catholic community of the Irvine Valley, who recently celebrated its centenary.

To All and Sundry

Whom these presents do or may concern, we, Sir Thomas Innes of Learney, Knight Commander of the Royal Victorian Order, Baron of Learney, Kinniardy and Yeochrie, Doctor of Laws, Advocate, Lord Lyon King of Arms, send Greetings; Whereas, The Provost, Magistrates and Councillors of the BURGH OF GALSTON in the County of Ayr have by Petition unto Us of date 18th November 1963 Shewn; THAT the said Burgh of Galston was erected to Burghal Status as from 9th May 1864 in terms of the General Police Improvement (Scotland) Act of 1862; THAT the Burgh is situated in the upper regions of the Valley of the River Irvine at its junction with the Burnawn Burn on land within the superiority of the Duke of Portland (who bears for his surname of Bentinck, Azure, a cross moline Argent) and had earlier associations with Sir William Keith of Galston who in 1331 brought home from Spain the heart of King Robert the Bruce, and with the Families of Lockart of Barr and Campbell of Cessnock; AND the Petitioners having prayed that there might be granted unto the said Burgh such Ensigns Armorial as may be found suitable and according to the Laws of Arms, KNOW YE THEREFORE, that We have Devised, and Do by These Presents Assign, Ratify and Confirm unto the Petitioners for and on behalf of the Burgh of Galston the following Ensigns Armorial, as depicted upon the margin hereof and matriculated on even date with These Presents upon the 91st. page of the 45th Volume of our Public Register of All Arms and Bearings in Scotland, Videlicet:— Per pale Dexter, Argent, a dexter hand in a steel gauntlet proper fessways, holding up a heart Gales, and on a chief Gales three pallets Or; Sinister, Azure, a cross moline Argent, on a chief Ermine two weavers' shuttles saltire wise azure, threaded Or, between as many escalops Gales, and in an Escrol below the Shield which is ensigned of a coronet befitting a Police Burgh (videlicet:— Azure, masoned Argent) is placed this Motto LABORE ET FIDUCIA, by demonstration of which Ensigns Armorial the said Burgh is amongst all Nobles and in all Places of Honour to be taken, numbered, accounted and received as an Incorporation Noble in the Noblesse of Scotland; IN TESTIMONY WHEREOF We have Subscribed these Presents and the Seal of Our Office is affixed hereto at Edinburgh this Twenty-seventh day of February in the Thirteenth Year of the Reign of Our Sovereign Lady Elizabeth the Second, by the Grace of God, of the United Kingdom of Great Britain and Northern Ireland and of Her Other Realms and Territories, Queen, head of the Commonwealth, Defender of the Faith, and in the year of Our Lord, One Thousand, Nine Hundred and Sixty-four.

THOMAS INNES OF LEARNEY.
LYON.

THE BURGH ARMS

In the 1950's and 60's the councils of the three towns of the Irvine Valley were informed that they were using unofficial coats-of-arms. Being sticklers for the right historical traditions and inclined to acquire the correct form, each made an application and was granted a new and official heraldic device with accompanying scroll. A reproduction of the wording on Galston's is shown here.

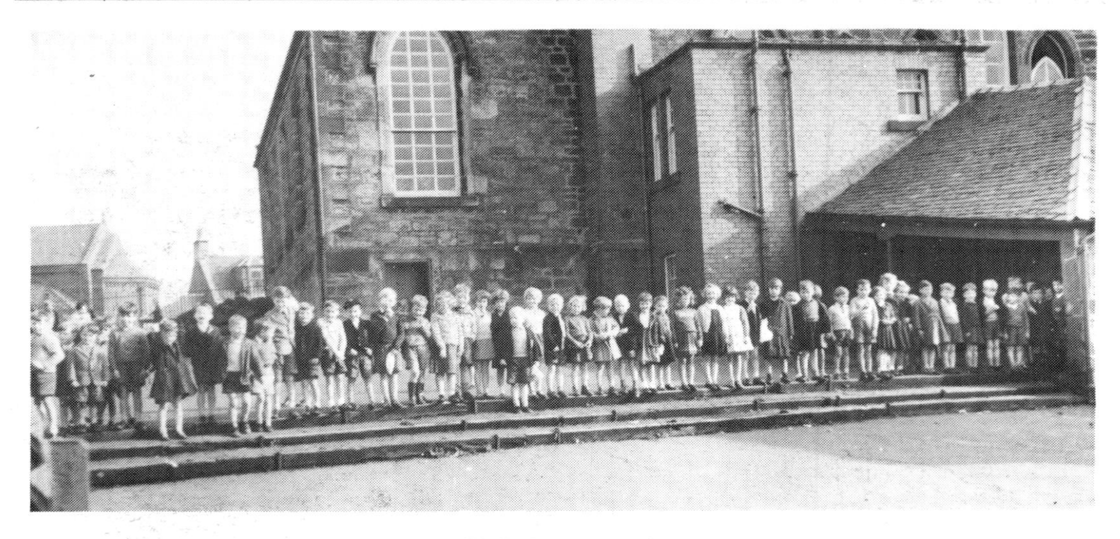

END OF AN ERA

The last classes at Barr School pictured here before it closed and all the primary children moved into the schools in Glebe Road. Built in 1859 in the same year as the Erskine Church, it served the children of the U.P. Church communicants until the Education (Scotland) Act of 1872 made separate parish or church schools unnecessary. The building is now used for community activities.

ODD ANGLES

Odd angles at the railway station before demolition. Underground workings of the mining industry have caused subsidence in places in and around the town. This can be clearly seen in this photograph taken in 1963, showing the platforms, the station offices, the houses in Duke Street and the dome of St. Sophia Church. The poster in the window displays the timetable of the trains from Kilmarnock, calling at Barleith, Galston, Newmilns and Darvel. The station was the centre of the town's commercial activity since the line was opened in 1848 to develop the mining industry. By 1963 it was a ghost of its former days and within a year the line was closed to passenger traffic.

DESIRABLE RESIDENCES

After a long inter-war and post-war period of council house construction, certain parts of the town proved attractive to private housing in the late 1960's and the 1970's. The largest area for this type of development lay between Station Road and Maxwood Road on or near the old railway track. Cessnock Place, shown here, occupies a similar site between Cessnock Road and Cemetery Road. Both areas add a new dimension and variety to the traditional appearance of the town. Beyond the fields, on the horizon, is Burnhousehill Farm.

BURGH WORKMEN

Between 1864 when it was created a burgh and 1975 and its loss of independence as a local government unit, Galston had its own workmen who maintained services in the town. They wholly or partly were responsible for lighting, sewerage, roads, cleansing, water supply and other essential duties. These were carried out under local supervision with a body of knowledge and information on the neighbourhood to assist them in their tasks. This photograph from the 1950's shows three members of the Cleansing Department snatching a minute from their tour of duty in New Road, namely Bobby Christie, John Samson and John Lynn.

GALSTON
BURGH BAND

1872 - 1972 ANNIVERSARY CONCERT

Assembly Hall, Loudoun Academy

Thursday, 9th November, 1972

ASSISTED BY

LOUDOUN ACADEMY SECONDARY GIRLS CHOIR

Band Instrumentation

Soprano Cornet	Jim Stewart
Principal Cornet	Willie Mitchell
Solo Cornet	Jim Allan
Solo Cornet	Jim Hunter
Solo Cornet	Walter Nisbet
Solo Cornet	John Allan
Flogel Horn	George Murray
Repiano Cornet	Jim Meek
2nd Cornet	George Findlay
2nd Cornet	George McLeod
3rd Cornet	Archie Parker
3rd Cornet	Davie Law
Solo Horn	John Stewart
1st Horn	John Ferguson
2nd Horn	George Ferguson
1st Baritone	John Grier
2nd Baritone	David Connell
Solo Euphonium	David Ferguson
Solo Euphonium	Ian Fairley
Solo Trombone	Robert Neil
1st Trombone	Arthur Frazer
2nd Trombone	John Head
Bass Trombone	Robin Brown
Eb Bass	George Paton
Eb Bass	Michael Gilmour
Bb Bass	Eric Dalziel
Bb Bass	David Reid
Percussion	Andrew Murray

THE OLD TRADITIONS

Every year another anniversary arrives of an event in the history of the town. In 1972 it was the centenary of the formation of the Burgh Band and a concert was held in Loudoun Academy with the assistance of the school's girls' choir. Although founded in 1872 and in continuous existence since then, an instrumental band of some kind is mentioned in the historical record almost fifty years earlier. Members of the Band at the time of the centenary are listed here as inheritors of a long tradition.

THE LAST FLOOD

The last flood in Galston occurred during the building of the long awaited by-pass road and bridge in 1978. Forecasts of possible danger by local spectators went unheeded with disastrous results. The picture shows the bottom end of the town once again inundated, when the interiors of houses in Titchfield Street were badly damaged and the green of the L.W.M. Bowling Club destroyed. The road to Kilmarnock and surrounding fields are covered by the floodwaters as the River Irvine has the final say.

OLD AND NEW

A large area of old Galston bounded by Brewland Street, Manse Place, Chapel Lane and New Road was demolished in the late 1950's and early '60's and replaced by the new flats and terraced houses seen here at the foot of Manse Brae. Recently a further development of private housing has been made on the right in the field between the Brae and John Knox Street.

SEEING IS BELIEVING

The Galston by-pass, mooted in the 1920's and surveyed soon after at last under construction in the late 70's. At the west end of the town the new bridge over the river Irvine is being built. Obstruction in the river caused the last serious flooding in the lower part of the town. In the middle ground is the L.W.M. Bowling Club and behind it the flats of Craigie Place.

A MODERN TOWNSCAPE

Much of the old part of the town to the west has been swept away. The old buildings in Standalane and the miners' rows in John Street and Boyd Street have disappeared. Some new parts of Galston would confuse returning natives, but the steeple of the parish church still dominates the town and is seen here in a recent print overlooking the new houses in Titchfield Street west of Orchard Street. In its rebuilding work the burgh council attractively merged the old with the new, and left to the district council the challenge of refurbishing the oldest, central parts of Galston and the other Valley towns.

GAS LANE

Gas Lane is another street in the town which has been transformed from an area of dereliction to a quiet residential place. On the left are the old premises of the Galston Co-operative Society and on the right modernised cottages. Along the riverside from Gas Lane to Bowling Green Lane, private houses have been built recently. In the background is Waterside Farm, better known over many years as Clachans farm. The gas holder and works by the river were demolished soon after the installation of North Sea gas.

INDUSTRIAL DEVELOPMENT

While west of the Muckle Brig has been allocated to residential housing, to the east in the old garden and orchard lands of Longhouse, new factories have been sited. This is an area of great change. What were once the lace and madras factories of Robertson's and Hendrie's are now occupied by different companies. Only the buildings of Longhouse seen in the right foreground remain familiar. On the left where Kilknowe Mill stood there is a row of modern factories. The stark gable end of the old Free Kirk, can be seen with a fresh new face under new owners, while the dome of St. Sophia's Church stands out in the background.

STEAM TRAINS

Steam trains called at Galston Station for over a century. No. 80049 was one of the last in July 1963. By this date there was no great crowd waiting to board for Newmilns and Darvel and a comfortable and leisurely form of travel disappeared forever from the Valley. Behind on the horizon is the farm of Burnhousehill otherwise known as Blue Braes. The station and track are now a built up area as Galston continues to push out into the countryside.

THE ROUNDABOUT

Not long after the trains stopped running, Galston lost most of its through traffic with the completion of the by-pass road north of the river. Motor transport could pass to Edinburgh, Glasgow and Kilmarnock, without touching the town, from this roundabout near the Muckle Brig. Time will tell what changes this will bring to the citizens of Galston as they approach the 21st century.

THE RIVER IRVINE

The River Irvine and its tributaries were the power source of the water mills which helped bring the Valley towns into existence and later supplied the steam engines of the lace factories. Now the river is chiefly a feature in the landscape. Children seldom swim or paddle in it, although it is still an attraction for anglers. West of the Muckle Brig it is once again a pleasant walk along both banks. This print shows the corner of the Loudoun Working Men's Bowling Green, the flats in Craigie Place and beyond the trees, the houses of the sheltered housing scheme of Ross Court.

THE OLD COUNCIL CHAMBER

The old council chamber of Galston Burgh council, with Provosts Kyle and Richmond looking down from the walls. Although the new municipal buildings had been erected as recently as 1926, the council had celebrated the centenary of the burgh in 1964. It proved the culmination of community life stretching back to the 12th century. After 1975 there was no longer a governing body of local men and women, as provosts, bailies and councillors, with their officials, to concern themselves with the affairs of the town. The council chamber fell silent forever, and the scenes that were enacted there live on only in old newspaper accounts, and in folk memory. A new era has begun and new organisations must face the test of time.

LABORE • ET • FIDUCIA